Qual-Online
The Essential
Guide

Qual-Online
The Essential Guide

What every researcher
needs to know about
conducting and moderating
interviews via the web

JENNIFER DALE AND
SUSAN ABBOTT

Paramount Market Publishing, Inc.

Paramount Market Publishing, Inc.
274 North Goodman Street, STE D-214
Rochester, NY 14607
www.paramountbooks.com
Phone: 607-275-8100

Publisher: James Madden
Editorial Director: Doris Walsh

This publication is designed to provide accurate and authoritative information in regard to the subject matter covered. It is sold with the understanding that the publisher is not engaged in rendering legal, accounting, or other profes-sional services. If legal advice or other expert assistance is required, the services of a competent professional should be sought.

All trademarks are the property of their respective companies.

ISBN 13: 978-1-941688-26-7 | ISBN 10: 1-941688-26-8

Contents

Chapter 1   Introduction   1

Chapter 2   History of Online Qual   5

Chapter 3   Exploring the Landscape   14

Chapter 4   Objectives, Methods, and Tools   45

Chapter 5   Ethical Considerations   67

Chapter 6   Calculating Costs   75

Chapter 7   Recruiting to Online Qual Studies   87

Chapter 8   Managing Online Qual Studies   96

Chapter 9   Real-Time Text Moderating Online   113

Chapter 10   Extended-Time Moderating Online   134

Chapter 11   Moderating Web Meetings   160

Chapter 12   Transcripts and Analysis   172

Chapter 13   Conclusion   189

Glossary of Terms   193

Acknowledgment   205

A Roadmap   207

About the Authors   209

CHAPTER 1

Introduction

[Welcome to the City of Insights!
May we show you around?]

Online qualitative research enlists a broad array of proven approaches that can no longer be labeled new or trendy. Established methods for gathering qualitative insights online have given social scientists the key to a great city! Online qual opens doors and invites candid, personal feedback from research participants in the safe, comfortable environment in which they live. The more we explore the growing landscape of online qualitative research, the greater our appreciation for the vast web network that makes all these communications possible.

However, there is a lot in the field that is new. As qualitative researchers experiment with new tools, we create new approaches. And while the tools themselves keep getting better, the technology that supports the tools continues to shine light on new and interesting avenues of exploration. More and more people around the world are connecting and communicating in cyberspace, reducing the sampling bias of years past. In fact, online qual ultimately brings more people in more places into the process, and is generally a democratizing influence in terms of participation.

The time seemed right to record the fundamentals; to create a resource of collected knowledge and provide a foundation for the exciting times to come.

Who This Book Is For

The core skills required to be a good Qualitative Research Consultant (QRC) are the same for online qualitative as they are for in-person research. Clear research objectives, an effective screening questionnaire, an unbiased discussion guide, and insightful analysis are the foundation of any good qualitative research study.

If you are new to your career in qualitative research, learning how to do online qualitative is a foundational skill, as important as learning how to do in-person research. Learning at least some of these approaches is a stepping stone to the new tools that will continue to come along.

If you're a seasoned QRC, congratulations! Whether you've ignored, dabbled-in or fully embraced online qualitative research, this book will help you. Looking five years ahead, it seems obvious to us that most researchers will be offering their clients new ways and new approaches using online methods. Don't be left behind with nothing to offer but old ideas and expensive pricing. Offering your clients the option of online qual is a way for you to welcome them into the future. This book will help you go forward with confidence, and we hope will give you a fresh spring in your step as you explore new territory in this expansive city.

We hope that the experienced online researcher will also find this book useful in a couple of different ways. We learned a great deal from each other in the process of writing it, as well as drawing on the experiences of our professional community. Most of us seem to start with one online methodology, either real time or extended, and focus most of our attention there. If that describes you, then this book will give you new insight into similar methods where you can build on your experience and expand your skills to master all the different approaches!

How to Navigate

Our brief history of online qualitative research is certainly not necessary reading, but we truly enjoyed our detective work in documenting the story, particularly the serendipity involved at every step of the way. The internet and everything connected to it has always been something of a crowd-sourced project, as you will see in **Chapter 2.**

The expansion in methodologies and modalities for research has created a situation where the boundaries are not as clear as they used to be. When we started to organize this material, we thought we had clarity. Then we realized we had a Venn diagram. Ultimately, we decided on the broad classifications set forth in **Chapter 3:** real time or extended; individual or group; modalities of communication and modalities of data collected. This simple approach should help you classify and deconstruct what's really going on with any new platform or approach you come across for online qual.

Classifications of that type felt a bit dry, though, so we thought we'd have a little fun. We started thinking of insights as a city to be explored and research methods as transportation. There are many possible destinations in the city of insights, and many ways to get there. Just think of Venice – you can arrive by plane, travel into the city on a bus or a car, have your luggage moved on a handcart, take the Vaporetto down the large canals and gondolas or motorboats down the small canals, or simply walk over the cobblestones. As you move around the city, there are big sights and little ones, large squares and tiny plazas, and seemingly an art-filled church every which way you turn. There is no one best way; there are many ways.

Chapter 4 starts to dig into specific tools and how you might use them. We have given you our thoughts about things to ask your platform provider so you have a good starting point.

Behaving in an ethical and responsible manner should be pretty straightforward, but there are a few potholes we all need to avoid. The growth in mobile methodologies means that we all need to rethink some of what we are doing to ensure we are treating our participants fairly and with respect. **Chapter 5** covers this territory, and points you to some other resources where you can learn more.

Because qualitative research is a business, you will need to figure out what things are going to cost. Just as with travel, or with face-to-face online research, it is easy to overlook something and get surprised when you mess up your budget. Read **Chapter 6** to be sure you haven't overlooked some essentials.

A persistent myth about online qualitative is that recruiting is different, or substandard in some way. In fact, recruiting to online qualitative studies is largely the same as face-to-face qualitative. We share some great tips with you that should make your journey more comfortable. This material is in **Chapter 7.**

There are always a lot of details to manage in any qualitative research event, and **Chapter 8** lays out a simple list of tasks to follow when conquering this seemingly daunting process. From getting your stimuli organized to ensuring your participants show up, this chapter is a goldmine of good information for designing and managing online qual studies.

Chapters 9, 10 and 11 are about actually designing and moderating in the three main types of platforms: real-time text chat, extended discussion forums, and real-time web-enabled interviews. There is necessarily some overlap here, but we've highlighted the important differences. If you have experience in one of these methods, we encourage you to branch out and try the others. You may be surprised what you already know.

Chapter 12 will take you through the deliverables phase of your project – how to deal with the data and how to get it all organized. Online qualitative can produce a daunting quantity of data filled with great stories and insights. While there are no silver bullets (we wish there were!), we do offer tips and suggestions for managing the bounty.

Chapter 13 wraps-up our tour and offers a few thoughts on what the future holds. That's a dangerous thing to do in this age of constant change, but there are some definite trends that we think will drive the development of online qual for a few years at least. (Or at least provide a future chuckle!)

There's also a **Glossary.** If you see a term that's not familiar, check there for a down-to-earth explanation.

Now that we've given you the overview, let's grab our luggage and our cameras and go exploring! You can start at the beginning or hop straight to the middle – the city of insights is at your feet. **Welcome!**

CHAPTER 2

History of Online Qual

[What did the early explorers encounter?]

The moment people could connect and communicate online, researchers were there. In the beginning the research was technical, paving the way for a vast network of open communication that was to follow. As this virtual network of people grew, marketing researchers strapped on their boots and began exploring new ways of mining and collecting data. It wasn't long before social researchers suited-up and started using email, group chats, and bulletin board systems to gather information. All of these initial efforts cleared the way for what is now known as online qualitative research.

Key Technologies Supporting Online Research

A number of important technology innovations support our work today; among them: packet data, routing protocols, IP addresses and URLs, TCP/IP communication protocols, file-sharing, Ethernet, wireless and mobile comput-ing, digital cellular networks, and many more. As with everything related to the internet, the history is a story of ground-up development. What follows is a brief tour of what we think are some interesting highlights.

While not specifically designed for research, the earliest binary communica-tion via a computer network occurred via a telephone line in 1965, thanks to an experiment by two pioneers at MIT, Lawrence G. Roberts and Thomas Merrill.

Although electronic computers were on the scene as early as the 1950s, they were not (yet) networked to communicate with each other. By 1969, a packet-switch network funded by the US Department of Defense, the Advanced Research Projects Agency Network (ARPANET), had connected four universities: University of California, Los Angeles; University of California, Santa

Barbara; Stanford; and University of Utah. Talented engineers supported by the US Government spurred the network's early progress and development, including email in 1972, Ethernet technology in 1973, the Computer Science Network (CSNET) in 1981, and the host protocol transition to TCP/IP in 1983, among others.

Advances in circuitry and other technologies fed the growth and eventual replacement of ARPANET by the National Science Foundation Network (NSF-NET) in 1985, thus providing government researchers and education organizations access to multiple supercomputers and networking centers.

The World Wide Web (WWW) was conceived and developed by Tim Berners-Lee, a British scientist working at CERN, the European Organization for Nuclear Research, in 1989. The goal was to enable easier sharing of information among scientists around the world. In 1993, CERN put the software for the WWW into the public domain, assuring widespread dissemination and free public access.

Timeline for Online Qualitative Reasearch
1990's

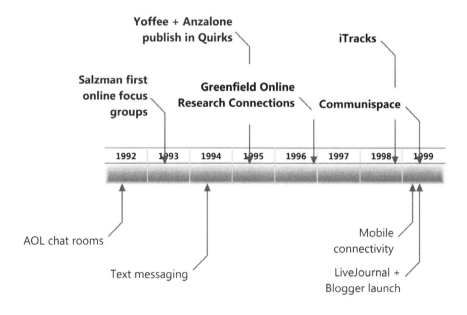

The first web site was hosted on Berners-Lee's NeXT computer, and provided instructions for making a website.

In 1991, the introduction of Hypertext and the first working online editor and browser came on board, followed by the introduction of Concurrent Versions System (CVS) for code management, which further enabled independent development. While the WWW was publicly available in 1991, early entrepreneurs encountered paralyzing communication restrictions until the NSFNET was decommissioned in 1995. (Barry M. Leiner, 2013; National Science Foundation, 2013). Internet Privatization, the first international WWW conference, and the awarding of network access contracts to commercial companies in 1995 opened the flood gates for providers and launched a new era of online communication and commerce.

The first mobile phone with internet connectivity was the Nokia 9000 Communicator, developed by Finland-based Nokia in 1996. NTT DOCOMO, a Japanese telecommunications company, launched the first mobile internet services platform in 1999. In 2001, Research In Motion brought email to your mobile phone. Text messaging on mobile phones followed the development of the Global System for Mobile Communications (GSM) network, beginning in Finland in 1994, spreading quickly through Europe, and then the US in 1996. Text messaging has very high penetration rates: more than 75 percent of mobile phone users in the US, and over 80 percent in Europe (2012 statistics.)

Just two thousand Internet-connected computers existed in 1985. By 2012, the number of individual internet users across the globe was estimated to be almost 2.5 billion (Internet World Stats, 2013). Cisco believes that in 2014, an estimated one hundred devices will connect to the internet every second. (Tillman, 2013) The internet is now a globally distributed network without a central governing body and incalculable future growth.

Pioneers in Online Qualitative

Prior to 1991, a few early adopting researchers were using private networks called Bulletin Board Systems (BBS) to conduct online qualitative research via typed text with one or more invited participants.

EARLY TRAVELER

Ricardo Lopez

In 1984 Ricardo Lopez was a young student at Syracuse University when he used one of the earliest forms of online qualitative research. With a new tool called a laptop and a 300 BPS modem, Lopez and his friends connected to a larger network of schools and communicated with other students on a virtual bulletin board using just text. Armed with the boards and his charm, Ricardo talked to girls across the country at UCLA, honing his online interviewing skills and unleashing a passion for technology.

A BBS is a computer system running software that allows users to connect and log-in to the system using a terminal program. Once logged in, a user can perform functions such as uploading and downloading software and data, reading news and bulletins, and exchanging messages with other users, either through electronic mail or in public message boards. Many early BBSs at the time also offered online games, in which users could compete with each other, and BBSs with multiple phone lines provided chat rooms, allowing users to interact with each other.

The first public dial-up BBS was developed by Ward Christensen. According to an early interview, while he was snowed in during the Great Blizzard of 1978 in Chicago, Christensen along with fellow hobbyist Randy Suess, began preliminary work on the Computerized Bulletin Board System, or CBBS. CBBS went online on February 16, 1978, in Chicago, Illinois.

Early BBSs were often a local phenomenon, as one had to dial into a BBS with a phone line and would have to pay additional long distance charges for a BBS out of the local calling area. Thus, users of a given BBS usually lived in the same area, and activities such as BBS Meets or Get-Togethers, where everyone from the board would gather and meet face-to-face, were common. As the use of the internet became more widespread in the mid- to late-1990s, traditional BBSs rapidly faded in popularity. Today, internet forums occupy much of the same social and technological space as BBSs did, and the term BBS is often used to refer to any online forum or message board. A classic BBS had: a computer; one or more modems; one or more phone lines; a BBS software package; a system operator; and a user community. (The BBS Corner, 2014)

EARLY TRAVELERS

Marian Salzman

While dozens of curious researchers explored the new on-line landscape, the first known person to contract a qualitative marketing research study among consumers online was Marian Salzman in 1992. Salzman saw early-on the advantages of connecting virtually with research participants. Back then she was President of BKG Youth and co-founder of Cyberdialogue, "the world's first online market research company," with Jay Chiat and Tom Cohen.

In the search for a more candid approach to survey taking, Salzman, a rising star in the advertising and research arena in the early 1990's, partnered with American On-Line (AOL) to build private chat rooms specifically for conducting online focus groups. Her existing research panel was invited to join AOL and in less than a few months Salzman was in high demand for her proprietary access to identifiable online consumers.

• • • • • •

Amy Yoffie and Marj Anzalone

In 1995, Amy Yoffie, President of Research Connections, and Marj Anzalone, President of Marj Anzalone Research (not pictured), conducted focus groups online using AOL chat rooms. The two published an article in *Quirks Marketing Research Review* a few months later, defending the methodology and detailing their early experience. The websites where they conducted the groups were public, requiring someone to monitor and ask "wanderers" who entered unexpectedly to leave. The authors also mentioned the convenience of clients "dialing-in" to watch the conversations from home, which was an extraordinary consideration at the time.

Yoffie went on to sell clients across the country on the benefits of online research and established herself as an early leader in the industry. In 1997, Jennifer Dale joined Yoffie in the development of a robust and proprietary web-based platform specifically designed for conducting online focus groups. The two discovered firsthand that not only were real-time discussions effective for collecting honest feedback, but also they were exciting for participants, the moderator, and even the clients. The energy, candor, and creativity online chats elicited opened the doors to a whole new world of qualitative research.

Development of Online Chat

Surprisingly, what held back rapid expansion in the business-to-consumer (B2C) market in those early days was not confirming identities of the participants (recruiting practices remained pretty much the same),); it was finding participants with online access, especially in the evenings. Like in-person focus groups, conducting online focus groups in the evenings is common. Across the U.S., for example, online groups that start at 7pm or 9pm Eastern accommodate participants after work across all time zones and have good show rates.

Although CompuServe was the first service to offer the general public internet connectivity and online chat (1980), they were slow to expand and were quickly overwhelmed by AOL's growth. AOL, which acquired CompuServe in 1997.

Before 1995, AOL held all the strings, as restrictions on the commercial use of the internet held back competition until the NSFNET was decommissioned. AOL's unstable and low-speed connections were of little concern. Its partnership with Salzman gave the company access to known consumers, whom it easily migrated to AOL, giving it the largest proprietary panel of research participants at the time.

While network connections were readily available to businesses in the early nineties, most individual consumers remained out of the loop without internet access at home. It took just a few years for AOL to expand and other internet service providers like Microsoft Network (MSN), EarthLink, and Prodigy were soon offering affordable connections to homes across North America.

Initially, recruiting for online groups was limited to those who were already using the technology, which included an abundance of males in the Information Technology (IT) field. As residential homes were asked to join and acquired internet access, the online population exploded and online qualitative research really hit the gas.

Being online and available wasn't the only cost-of-entry into an online focus group. Participants had to have a working email address and know how to "copy the URL" and "open their browser." Staffing the Help Desk phone in the early years of online qual was a front row seat to a changing culture.

Teenage girls reviewing a new makeup website, avid readers giving feedback on a new book store concept, high-end car buyers reviewing new designs, and women revealing their personal experiences with menopause – qualitative researchers like Susan Roth at Greenfield Online and Mary Beth Solomon at BKG Youth were getting it all.

"In the beginning, online focus groups were limited to just text, and you had to be able to type really fast. Once we could test visuals and not have to type every question in the discussion guide, live moderating got a lot easier."
– Mary Beth Solomon, Developmental Psychologist
BKG Youth, 1993-1997

The early years offered relatively slow connection speeds and limited devices to access the internet, which created a ripe environment for the growth of low bandwidth, text-based interviews in real-time and extended time. Pioneering researchers looked for new tools to capture the full potential of this emerging qualitative research methodology, and entrepreneurial developers quickly responded to the increased demand.

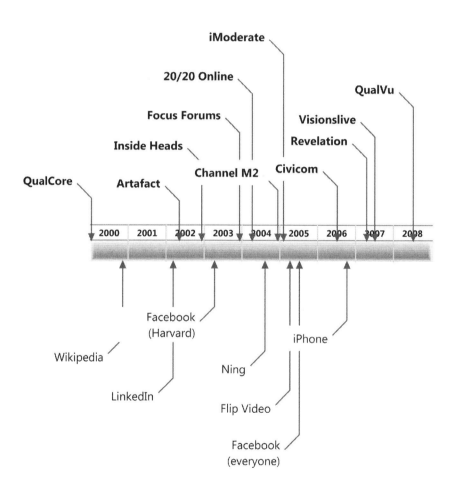

Timeline for Online Qualitative Reasearch
selected launches, 2000's

Continued Growth

During the early 2000s, significant expansion in online qualitative research applications occurred. Bulletin board systems were adapted for commercial use by a growing number of firms serving the research community. As people everywhere started interacting more online, the growth of online community software created an interest in using similar features for research purposes.

The rise of the smartphone and desire for mobile access are driving development of innovative platforms that make use of the built-in functionality of the phones, such as geo-location and cameras. The future is not yet written, but it will surely include technology to that will further enable qualitative researchers.

In the next chapter, we'll take you on a tour of the online qual landscape. The city of insights is what we're calling it, where there are many places of interest, methods of travel, and routes you can take. Come aboard!

CHAPTER 3

Exploring the Landscape

[Will you be taking the limo or the scooter?]

There are so many forms of online qualitative, you may find yourself overwhelmed by all the choices. Using our transportation analogy, there are a lot of different ways to explore the landscape. Limousines are luxurious and fully equipped, but expensive. A Segway scooter can take you places that a larger vehicle can't go. If you have a lot of people with you, you might choose a tour bus or even a highway bus. There are cars and balloons and gondolas, and there's always the option of just getting out there on foot! Like any vehicle, once you get to know what one looks like, you will see similarities. All the different sedans, coupes, and mini-vans in a showroom are still automobiles at the core. You'll notice familiar looking features, like tires, engines, seats, and steering wheels.

In this section, we will be talking about platforms, but we never want to lose sight of the fact that research is a journey. You don't come home from Paris and tell people all about the tour bus; you come home and tell them the places you saw and the people you met. Research is all about the learning. A balloon ride might be pretty cool, but only if you want to look at things from above.

Let's go look at the showroom, and get a feel for some of the types of research transportation tools that can take you to that great city of insights.

Synchronous or Asynchronous
[Real time or extended time]

One big difference you will see in types of methodology has to do with the dimension of time. Synchronous methodologies all happen at the same time. The research event is scheduled in terms of a start time and an end time just like any meeting or focus group. Duration of the group is measured in minutes or hours and you need to consider time zones. For our purposes, we will refer to this as **real time**.

Time Dimension

Real Time
(aka synchronous)

Extended
(aka asynchronous)

Asynchronous approaches are scheduled as well, but usually in terms of days or weeks or even longer. Imagine a room with pieces of flipchart paper up on the walls, and markers nearby. The researcher comes into the room and writes a question or topic at the top of each flipchart, then leaves. Then the participants come and go over the next several hours or days, writing their own additions to the flipcharts. It's like a discussion in slow motion. Duration of the group is measured in days or weeks. We will refer to this as **extended time.**

This distinction is an important one, and will affect the design of the project in significant ways. All of these methods do have one important thing in common: they will let you conduct research with someone who is not in the same room as you, and perhaps not or even in the same country.

Individual or Group

A second dimension that distinguishes some approaches is whether the interaction is one-on-one (an in-depth interview) or a group discussion. Both of these approaches can be ported into the online world. The two may seem distinct; however they are not. Some online methodologies will let you have the best of both worlds, running individual activities like online journals in parallel with a group discussion, for example. As you come to understand the strengths and weaknesses of different approaches, you will see that the rules of face-to-face research don't always apply.

Interaction Dimension

One on One
Interview

Group
Discussion

Modes of Interaction + Types of Data Collected

On any project, you as the moderator may be communicating through a variety of modes, including voice (live or recorded), text, video (live or recorded), and images. You may be testing stimuli in one or more of these modes. And you may be collecting data from participants in one or more of these modes.

Types of Data Collected

Video   Audio   Group

Photos, Images, Markups   Text Discussion Documents

In practice, there are platforms that pull these types of interactions together. Not all platforms include all modes of communication, and some are real time and some are extended. These distinctions are quickly evaporating as platforms keep adding features.

Platforms Pull It All Together

Online Focus Group (Real Time Text)

Web-enabled Interview or Group

Mobile Platform Mobile Access

Community Platform

Next up on our tour is a visit to a few of these modes, starting with the one that is closest to face-to-face: talking in real time.

Talking in Real Time

Consider the idea of people simply talking as a foundation of qualitative research. You can talk one-on-one (an interview) or as a group (a focus group). Both of these methods can be done by telephone – that long-ago innovation in talking technology!

Telephone

The telephone focus group has been a tried and true method for many years. As a basic method the telephone is still a great tool, and now comes in online and mobile versions too.

Using a conference calling service, you can have multiple people on the call. You might have silent observers from the client team listening from a muted phone. You might have a note-taker listening or be recording the call for later transcription. You may even have a live interpreter on the line if the conversation is in a language the observers don't understand.

Considerations

- Works very well for individual depth interviews (IDIs).
- Groups of two or three (dyads and triads), or even as many as six people (for some moderators) work well. Beyond six people, there is less air time for individuals, and the logistics become more difficult to manage.
- Accessible to almost anyone, almost anywhere, including hard-to-reach targets, like those who are homebound, children, and busy executives.
- People are comfortable talking on the phone and need no special training or equipment.
- Very cost effective method.
- Immediate and real-time.
- Requires a high skill level to manage group dynamics with no visual cues.

- There is no ability to present visual stimuli.
- If clients are listening in remotely, conversing privately with the moderator requires an added text or instant-messenger feature.

There are several ways of using online tools to add capabilities or richness to the conversation or the interview.

Adding Visual Stimuli

A major shortcoming of voice alone is not being able to show any visual stimuli. You might have concepts that are too long to read, advertising visuals, even video that you want to show. There are workarounds, of course. You can email something out in advance, or send someone to a website. But as the researcher, you have little to no control of the stimuli if you go that route.

Fortunately, adding the presence of visual stimuli during a telephone session has become a simple matter. Your options include: low cost internet calling services offering a screen-sharing option or web meeting services. Both can be simple or complex. Look for ones that will give you the flexibility to invite participants, load in some images or video, and show a variety of visual stimuli to an individual or a group. Some also offer recording and editing tools, an interactive whiteboard, polling questions, and chat windows.

· · · · · ·

MINI CASE STUDIES
Executive interviews to test creative concepts

A client wanted to test print advertising with senior executives in a wide variety of industries, including mining and fisheries companies that were remote. The advertising treatments were put into a PowerPoint deck and loaded into the online meeting platform. Using operator-assisted conference calling, we were able to have representatives from the client as well as the agency listen in to calls as they occurred. Immediately following the calls, the operator un-muted the observers for an instant debrief.

The cautionary tale here is that the schedule and budget we were planning allowed for a twenty-minute call after every interview, which spilled into the time we were planning to use for organizing notes, and taking a quick bio break. As well, the additional operator time added to the budget fieldwork costs for the project. However, the client loved the approach, which had tremendous immediacy, and which also allowed for iterative changes in our approach over the course of the interviews, including removing some concepts and adding others.

Pro tips: Build more than one version of the presentation deck so that you can easily rotate concepts and avoid order bias. Consider client debriefs in your scheduling and budgeting.

· · · · · ·

Student intern groups

A large organization wanted to include some summer interns in a larger research project. We were conducting research with the summer interns working for a large business. Face-to-face group discussions were held at the head office, but the client also wanted to include some students from other offices, even though there was no budget for travel. The solution was to hold a telephone focus group with web stimuli using a web-meeting platform. What we did not anticipate was that students in one city organized themselves to be in a meeting room all together in the remote location, rather than (the anticipated situation) each on their own telephone line with their own computer and keyboard. This significantly changed the group dynamics. The student interns were all on one phone speaker in one city, and the researcher was on another line in another city. This necessitated some on-the-spot rethinking, but the approach worked well, and was easy to add to the other planned fieldwork. And we had to rethink some of the exercises on the spot so they could do them as a group. However, we learned what we needed to learn, and all ended happily!

Adding Live Video

An additional level of intimacy can be achieved using real time video to complement the voice-to-voice interview or group discussion. Access to video cameras either through a webcam or a mobile device is rapidly becoming commonplace. The moderator can be the only one on video, while participants respond via audio or text, or participants can also be on video, along with the moderator.

TRAVEL TIP   A webcam by any other name

You may hear something called a webcam interview or webcam group, but it is equally likely that you will be interacting with people who are using the capabilities of their handheld devices. Focus on the type of interaction you are planning rather than the technology as such, because the technology is constantly shifting.

If you are dealing with a tech-savvy target group, and you are on a budget, you might choose to conduct a video interview using low-cost web meeting tools. With a bigger budget, you might choose a more robust platform with recording features, screen share, audio and text chat, breakout rooms, editing capability, etc. Virtual research facilities may use these same platforms, or have their own proprietary platform to conduct the interviews. Most professional facilities will offer you more support through the whole process. We will talk more about the kind of support you might want in Chapter 8.

Real-time video of participants brings some additional richness to the event. Because you can see the participants' surroundings, their immediate environments are more available to you. Individual research participants can show you things, either by holding them up to the camera, or by moving the camera (the whole laptop sometimes!).

Another advantage of having participants on video when compared with voice alone is that it pretty much forces the individual participants to pay attention to the conversation or interview, and not drift into watching their email or some similar distraction.

The size of your webcam group is limited by how many people can be interviewed effectively at one time, all sharing video communication. Chapter 8 discusses group size and duration considerations. Chapter 11 discusses moderating in real time using these kinds of platforms.

· · · · · ·

MINI CASE STUDY: Webcam interviews around the world

When you have a low incidence population that is widely dispersed, an online approach just makes sense. For this project, we used webcams to interview individuals in several countries about a uniquely expensive hobby they shared. It was a fascinating project, and having access to faces was very helpful in understanding attitudes, motivations, and context. Several of the interviewees chose to do the interview using their mobile phones for the scheduled call. In one case, the young man was in a rather noisy coffee café! Mobile-phone audio connections overseas were somewhat fuzzy, and the video was also less crisp in some cases. However there was no problem maintaining connections with any of the interviewees. The client team was able to observe some calls as they occurred, and watched others from the recordings. While it worked, the connections were sometimes noisy and made it hard to hear.

➲ PRO TIP: Anticipate that participants will use a mobile device to connect. If you want them at home or in a quiet environment, you should be clear about that expectation. If internet bandwidth will be a constraint, real-time video might not be your best choice.

TRAVEL TIP   What clients like about video

In a webinar sponsored by QRCA, a researcher and client discussed their experience of web video versus in-person interviews. Here were a few of the points noted by the clients in their experience of the webcam sessions:

- Clients could hear and see more clearly than from the back room.
- Respondents were more at ease. They needed less time to open up and shared more intimate details up front. They were relaxed in their own homes.

- There was additional functionality, like polls, whiteboards, and markup tools.

- There were some stimulus limitations; you lose the senses of touch, taste, and smell. You could perhaps ship product to participants.

- Other family members can be in the picture, such as dogs, etc. This adds an ethnographic component to the research, showing you what the participant's life is really like.

Modes of Interaction and Types of Data Collected by Methodology

Online Qualitative Methodology – Common Name	Primary Comm. Channel	Moderator Communicates via	Participants Communicate via	Timing	Duration of Data Collection
Bulletin Board Groups	Internet	Text, with possible Audio/Video components	Text, with possible Audio/Video components	Extended	Over several days or weeks
Chat Groups	Internet	Text, with possible Audio/Video components	Text, with possible Audio/Video components	Real	1-2 hours
Webcam Groups	Internet	Video & Audio (possibly text)	Video & Audio (possibly text)	Real	1-2 hours
Online IDIs	Internet	Video & Audio (possibly text)	Video & Audio (possibly text)	Real	15-30 minutes
Online Diaries-	Internet or Cellular	Instructions via Text, Video and/or Audio	Text, Video and/or Audio	Extended	Over several days or weeks
Email and/or SMS Messaging	Internet or Cellular	Text	Text	Real or Extended	Varies from short to extended periods
Social Media Listening	Internet	None	Text and Video	Extended	Varies
Mobile Interviews	Internet or Cellular	Text, Audio or Video	Text, Audio or Video	Real	10-30 minutes
Mobile Ethnography	Internet or Cellular	Text, Audio or Video	Text, Audio or Video	Real or Extended	Varies
Insight Communities	Internet	Text, Audio or Video	Text, Audio or Video	Real or Extended	Ongoing for several months or years

Online Focus Group / Text Chat

Chat groups or online focus groups (OLFG) are the online cousin to in-person focus groups. Like face-to-face interviews, chat groups are scheduled at a specific time for a short duration (typically 1 to 2 hours). The conversation among all participants and the moderator occurs simultaneously in real time. The text discussion appears on the screen and scrolls (up or down, depending on the platform) as new posts appear.

If you've ever used an instant messaging program or tried to get online help by clicking the "chat now!" button on a website, you have a basic idea how it works. Two or more persons are in a virtual environment able to respond simultaneously via text in real time. Research chat facilities are built with the moderator's needs in mind and will offer you loads of features and controls to capture feedback from multiple people who are all talking at the same time.

More than synchronous, chat is actually multi-synchronous. You can collect considerably more data from a text group than from the same number of people in face-to-face focus groups, and do it in less time.

The moderator has complete control of who has access to the room, the questions that are asked, the stimuli displayed on the whiteboard, and observers hidden from participants in the back room. Chat conversations are lively and the scrolling text conveys energy. Real-time chat is both dynamic and non-judgmental, making the methodology popular among researchers digging for insights on sensitive or personal topics.

The immediacy and relative low labor cost of chat groups make them popular among both moderators and clients. Clients can log-in to the virtual focus facility from anywhere there is an internet connection to observe the groups. Immediately following the discussion, transcripts are available and ready for analysis. Chapter 9 discusses moderating text chat in detail.

The "extras" you can incorporate in a text-chat environment are immeasurable when you consider that the stimuli you show to the group for immediate feedback can be anything on the web. The stimuli can be something you up-load, like a picture, text or a video, or a live website. It is the latter that makes a chat tool in real time so versatile. Not only can you ask participants to navigate a live website and report on their experience, **any web page you create** can be displayed to the group for input. Each participant in a chat group experiences the stimuli on his or her own monitor individually, yet sees the entire conver-sation on the screen.

TRAVEL TIP   Chat's versatility

Obviously you want to understand the unique features of the platform you are using, but there's probably a solution if you think creatively:

- Online survey tools can become poll questions. Randomize the answer choic-es and you have a customizable sorting exercise!
- Heat mapping and click tracking tools can be layered on to websites to which you have private access for additional metrics during an online focus group.
- Upload stimuli to a platform that allows for markups and display **that** link instead of the stimuli directly.
- Set up a live feed from your own webcam so participants can see and hear you when you choose.
- Eye-tracking software can be used to collect even **more** data from partici-pants in chat groups.

While we'll discuss the details of these tools and features later, here's a taste of what a chat facility specifically built for research may offer you:

- Full control over who sees what and for how long.
- Access for an assistant or back-up moderator with similar controls.
- Ability for observers to view the discussion in the virtual "backroom" without being seen by participants, while still being able to communi-cate with the moderator.
- Ability to see who is active in the room and identify who has not responded to the last question.

- Display of many different types of stimuli, both fixed and interactive.
- Ability to select screener information about participants for observers.
- Analysis tools that let you tag or mark comments, filter responses, and download full or partial transcripts in multiple formats.
- Live administrative features, like private messaging, booting, blinding and muting participants.
- Pre-loaded discussion guide questions.
- Participant features like anonymous user names, text responses, emoticons, and limited private messaging.
- Facility testing and pre-group access.
- Multiple language capability.
- Live interpreters via audio.
- Control over whether or not participants can edit their posted responses, respond more than once to a question, or read and respond to what others have posted.

Considerations

- Can capture immediate feedback in real time in less than two hours. It is possible for the moderator to react on the fly and change direction during a live group, either on her own or prompted by a client request.
- Easily handles multi-media stimuli ranging from imagery, links to web-sites, audio, and video. Superior control over group effects compared with face-to-face groups.
- Every participant responds at the same time to each question, reducing the herd mentality, a common challenge in any group discussion.
- Group sizes of 15 to 20 work well for most discussions, as smaller groups will feel slow for participants and larger groups can create too much text to read before it scrolls off the screen.
- Studies can include those who are hard of hearing or speaking, or phys-ically less able to get to a central location.
- Accommodates participants and clients with a fixed event scheduled in advance.
- A group discussion can easily occur with participants across multiple time zones simultaneously.
- Can provide full anonymity.

- Allows for immediate responses to questions and stimuli, which can be especially helpful when seeking top of mind or initial reactions to advertising and marketing materials.

. . . . . .

MINI CASE STUDIES
Website evaluation

A professional medical website was attracting an increasing number of consumers and the client didn't know why. Participants were recruited from the client's website and directed to an online screener. Eligible respondents were contacted via email and asked to visit and review three new websites before participating in the focus group. Recruits were contacted by phone and asked basic questions about the websites before being invited to participate in an upcoming group chat.

Six online focus groups were held. The design, layout, and content of the client's site was reviewed and compared with three other medical websites. Respondents were asked why they seek medical information online and how useful they found the information on the three websites visited.

The client decided to develop a consumer-oriented medical website as a direct result of the research findings. After creating a prototype of the site, another set of focus groups was conducted. Those who previously completed the screener, but were not invited to participate in the original set of groups were contacted via email to identify availability to participate in the new wave of groups. Participants in the second phase were shown images to reflect layout and documents to discuss content. Proposed features also were presented and participants interacted and commented about their experiences in real time. The insights gathered from those discussions were used to develop the final site, which was successfully launched a few months later.

. . . . . .

Brand positioning

A global candy manufacturer was looking to strengthen its brand positioning and develop an online game designed to promote the brand through character adventures. The client sought feedback on the overall gaming concept, as well as three distinct digital characters. With an end-user target market under age 13, The FTC's Children's Online Privacy Protection Act (COPPA) standards were strictly followed and parents of children age 9-12 were contacted and written permission from each parent was obtained before instructions to participate were sent.

Groups were segmented by age and gender and were scheduled to last one hour. Parents were instructed to observe and intervene if the child did not want to continue for any reason. Parents were also asked to type their child's responses if the child found the chat too overwhelming.

During the groups, children were shown each of the three characters in various situations and asked about their thoughts and feelings of each. While we expected limited typing skills from all groups, the 11- to 12-year-olds were very comfortable typing and willing to chat beyond the hour limit. While spelling errors were rampant, sentiment was not lost. The younger children, age 9-10, were surprisingly chatty as well, using emoticons and simple text expressions like "ewwwwwwww" to clearly convey their opinions throughout the discussion. Out of all six groups, only one child did not complete the discussion and only one child had his parent type his responses for him.

The client received a full report detailing the reactions from each gender and age set to the proposed characters and ultimately decided not to invest in developing new characters for the brand.

· · · · · ·

Market messaging

A regional home repair company held a long-term leadership position in the marketplace. The company was looking to update its marketing materials and wanted to get feedback from customers.

Because a limited number of customer email addresses were available, participants were recruited from the company's customer mailing list via postcard invitation. Willing customers were asked to phone or email the research company and answer a short screening questionnaire. Recruiting continued for a period of two weeks until both groups were filled. Twenty-five qualified respondents were invited via email to attend the discussion. The email invitation included a link to the online discussion and their assigned username. Phone calls were made to each invited participant on the day of the group.

Two groups were held in one evening and the company's marketing team observed remotely from their office. During the groups participants were asked about their relationship with the company and shown various images to represent different moods and feelings. The moderator probed responses to uncover the emotional connection between the customer and the repair company. As a result of the research the company was able to reprioritize its marketing messages and ultimately improve customer communication.

Talking Over Extended Time

There are many ways to connect in extended time. Discussion topics and research activities are created and launched in an environment that permits participants to come and go on their own schedule. As the moderator or the participant, each time you log in you will see new information, which might be new topics or new contributions (often called posts) from other participants.

Discussion Forum / Bulletin Board

The nature of how we each experience the internet individually supports conducting qualitative research over time. The discussion forum or bulletin board format is another pioneer method in online qualitative that is still going strong. The name comes from the early days of the internet. Bulletin Board Systems allowed users to connect by dialing-in, and then post or read messages, download software, and use electronic mail. The bulletin board terminology stuck, but decades of technology development has given us something much richer and better described as a discussion forum.

If you have ever seen a threaded discussion online, in a tech-support forum or on a social media site, you have seen something very much like a research discussion forum. Public discussion forums are stripped down compact cars with no power steering and no climate control, compared with the purpose-built research tools, which drive like luxury cars and have almost as many options. Professional discussion forum platforms put you as the researcher in a well-equipped cockpit, with many useful controls.

Success in using this approach depends on careful event design. Changing direction on the fly can be done, but not nearly as easily as in the real time methods. The best results occur when the moderator is able to build rapport and connection with the participants, which can be time-intensive during the early days of a study. This topic is explored further in Chapter 10.

We'll be talking more about the specific tools in other sections, but here are a few of the cockpit controls that distinguish the professional discussion forum platform from public forums:

- Full control over who sees what, including the ability to show some topics to only some segments or individuals.
- Ability to create observers that cannot be seen – the virtual "backroom," as well as create posts to this group.
- Quickly and easily see which posts are new and which participants have answered which questions, or even when a given individual was last active.
- Use of many different types of stimuli, including text, multi-media, markup tools or whiteboards, mini-polls, and others.
- Analysis tools that let you tag or mark the transcript, filter responses, and download full or partial transcripts in multiple formats.
- Participant profile tools that can attach an avatar or photo to all posts, can hide or show a name (or even assign an anonymous ID), give you a quick look at recruiting specs, and even show a map location reference.
- Platforms available in multiple languages, responsive to time zones, and on-board translation capabilities.
- Control over whether or not participants can edit their posted responses, respond more than once to a question, or read what others have posted.

Considerations

- Can capture experiences over an extended time period ranging from days to weeks or longer. It is possible to "interrupt" a project, enabling before and after approaches to any topic ranging from shopping to vacations.
- Easily handles multi-media stimuli ranging from imagery, links to web-sites, audio, video. Superior control over group effects compared with face-to-face groups.

- Permits participants or the moderator to share files, ranging from photos and documents to videos.

- Every participant can respond at the same time, and to all questions.

- Group sizes of 15 to 20 work well for most consumer topics. Smaller groups tend to feel a bit too quiet, and larger groups can create too much reading time for everyone.

- Accessible to everyone who can type their responses, or have someone else help them type their responses. Some visually impaired people can navigate text questions with their computer's text reader. Those who are deaf or hard of hearing or speaking, or physically less able to get to a central location can be included in a study.

- Can accommodate participant schedules very easily, regardless of their personal schedule (e.g., working nights) or location (in a different time zone).

- Can provide full anonymity.

- Permits a considered response, where a question is read, then answered one or more times after a period of thinking. This can be helpful when you want an in-depth response, but potentially problematic when you really want a top-of-mind quick reaction.

· · · · · ·

MINI CASE STUDIES
Boards for active lifestyles

A watch manufacturer was developing a new product for sports-minded, physi-cally active adults. Participants were screened to identify high interest in wear-able technology as well as a personal commitment to fitness. Bulletin board dis-cussions were used to accommodate the varied schedules of participants, as well as to better understand individual fitness routines over seven days. Segmented by age and gender, the online forums allowed participants to respond via text, photo and video, fostering rich feedback and offering great insight into what cus-tomers really needed.

· · · · · ·

Detailed feedback from professors

A publisher was interested in obtaining feedback on its undergraduate-level tax textbook prior to creating a new edition. Each university and college had only a few professors teaching the subject, so a discussion forum format offered the perfect solution to bring a far-flung and low-incidence group together. The discussion forum also offered opportunities for considered reflection and posting of detailed feedback, exactly what the client needed for this project. Some participants volunteered to upload examples of teaching presentations, providing a new source of insight. An "anything goes" section of the forum let this group connect with each other to discuss shared problems and concerns, providing further insight into their world and their challenges. The extended time format allowed time for questions to come up from participants, with answers assembled from the client project team posted later to the forum. Participants also canvassed their departmental peers on some of the ideas proposed, effectively including the opinions of people not in the actual study.

Blogs, Diaries and Journals

Paper diaries have long been used in marketing research, and this type of task ports very well to the online environment. The key difference between the electronic format and the paper version is the simplicity of monitoring the data capture as it occurs, and even asking follow-up or clarification questions immediately. No transcription is required, of course.

Another important difference with electronic journals is the ready ability to incorporate digital photos or videos as part of the exercise, or even the whole activity.

These terms tend to be used somewhat interchangeably, but in general, a journal or a diary is a one-to-one method, where only the researcher and the participant are interacting. Some blog environments can be set up to permit other respondents to see and react to what is being posted, creating more of a sense of social media and community.

As with other methods, free and low-cost tools can be used for this purpose.

A journaling tool is frequently an option with an online discussion forum. At its most basic, a threaded discussion where all questions are set up in a one-on-one format (fully blinded from all other participants) is a journal.

The difference in using a built-for-that-purpose tool is the ease of moderating it; participants' responses are separate, rather than all flowing together, for example.

A study can be arranged to combine a diary with a group discussion in many online discussion forum platforms.

Considerations

- Ideal for capturing instances of a recurring series of events, such as daily habits (e.g., daily eating, meal preparation, media use, dog walking).
- Ideal for capturing an extended event (e.g., wedding planning, home purchase, vacation experiences).
- Can be text only, or also include video or photographs.
- Questions may be the same for each day, or vary on a planned sequence.
- Easily extended into the mobile environment to permit out-of-home capture of activities.

· · · · · ·

MINI CASE STUDIES
A diary a day

As part of an ongoing ethnography study, a vitamin retailer sought to understand how people attempt to improve their own health and nutrition. Panel members were randomly selected and invited to complete a daily diary for one week. Fifty panel members agreed to participate in the added activity and 32 submitted entries each day via an online form. Daily entries included an assessment of their food intake as well as thoughts about their current health and fitness. Participants were not asked to modify their behavior, simply record their everyday actions and feelings. Diary respondents continued to participate in study activities with the rest of the panel over the next year, which included exposure to multiple articles and videos about health and nutrition. Six months after completing the diary exercise, twenty-nine respondents were interviewed individually by phone about their current thoughts and intentions for living a healthy lifestyle. Knowing how respondents felt months earlier, we were able to identify changes in attitude and behavior and discuss the possible impact of the stimuli they received.

. . . . . .

Blog exploration

A study of convenience store users started with a simple blogging exercise. Participants who were recruited for in-person groups noted their interactions with convenience stores during the week prior to their scheduled focus group discussion. Posts came in through a variety of means, including text messages, email, and from their computers, all going in to a simple blogging platform.

During the groups, the results of the advance blogging activity allowed the moderator to gently challenge participants on differences in stated behaviors versus those previously reported in their diaries, such as stopping for junk food versus healthy options, and as well as lottery ticket purchasing habits. The two methods complemented each other, and provided a much richer exploration of activities as well as attitudes, and how these interplay.

. . . . . .

Activity Based Versus Community Platforms
[What's the difference, really?]

As you journey into the city of insights, at times it can be tricky to figure out what kind of transportation device you are really looking at, and the marketing language used doesn't always help.

Activity-based platforms are similar in many ways to discussion forums, where there are threaded discussions, journaling activities, and multi-media question options. Community platforms seem almost the same at first glance; there are threaded discussions, multi-media capabilities, and so forth. The differences can be subtle, but here is how we see it.

Discussion forums feel a bit like a pleasure boat moving down a river, with people coming and going from their cabins, but often being in the same place together. Today we are looking at a castle, and tomorrow we are doing a shore excursion. Different question types and participant activities are attached to this basic directional flow.

Activity based platforms – even though the technology underpinnings are practically the same – feel more like a bicycle tour group, where individuals or small groups may peel off and do other things, then rejoin the group at the end of the day. Cyclists tick off the sights on the tour, tracking their own progress using the built-in tools. If they are too slow, they might find a museum closed when they get there, unless the moderator makes a special arrangement to keep it open for them. The individual research activities feel more isolated, even though they are connected to a larger theme in the study. It's a little bit choppier, but respondents may experience the environment as having more visual variety.

One result of this difference is that the need for active moderation may be somewhat reduced with activity-based platforms. Participants get a lot of reinforcement directly from the platform. The flip side is that there may be less of a sense of being part of an extended group discussion. And the more complex the activity-based platform, the more time must be allowed for people to become familiar with the environment. As the tools continue to evolve, we will increasingly see the best of both worlds.

Activity Based Platforms and Discussion Groups

Similar tools, organized differently

Participants see **activities**. A threaded discussion may be one of the activities

When participants enter, they see **discussions**. Activities are inside discussions

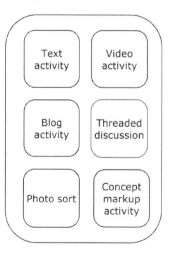
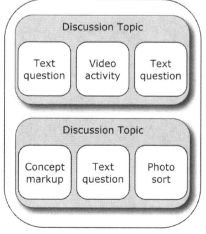

Community platforms are similar again, but can accommodate many more passengers. Consider a cruise ship that has hundreds or even thousands of passengers versus a sailing vessel with dozens. The cruise ship is set up so that most people pretty much find their own way from the pool to meal times. The captain knows how many people went on shore excursions today, but didn't talk to all of them personally. The small ship experience is one where the captain is talking to every passenger every day, sometimes multiple times a day, changing direction based on feedback, stopping to explore an unexpected cove. The focus is very much on what each participant says, not the aggregate of a large number of responses.

Community oriented platforms generally let participants start their own topics. This is essential in order to keep people engaged over long periods of time, without wearing out the moderator(s). Those that are built to support very large groups can feel almost quantitative in their orientation, as of course they are. They still permit drilling down to individual responses on any question if desired. Analytical tools start to become essential in this environment if one is not to be drowned in data. But enough drowning for now, let's get back on the boat and keep exploring the city of insights.

Video Based Platforms

Adding video into an extended discussion forum is pretty straightforward. Many platform options are available to you. At one time, and not all that long ago, you might have sent a small hand-held video camera to your participants by mail. Now, you are more likely to simply screen for video capabilities at the recruiting stage. Be aware of potential bias in your sample towards ownership of a particular tech device.

When we talk about video capabilities, we are not talking about a big camera. In fact, you actually do not want people using a fancy video camera because they will send you files that are large, and may also be longer than you want, or in a format that has to be converted. You really just want the video quality that is readily available from someone's mobile device or computer web camera.

Participants can usually add their videos into the platform in one of two ways. One way is to capture a video, save it, then upload it. The second option is to use the video capture capabilities built into the research platform. This typically means simply clicking on a "camera" icon, which will launch a video capture window using the camera on the participant's computer.

Video can also be used very effectively for asking questions, providing welcome messages, introducing new topics, and just building rapport between the researcher and the participants. A few research platforms have been designed with video as the primary tool of data collection, and include relatively sophisticated clipping and editing tools. Even one-way moderator video can add intimacy by introducing a personal element to the communication.

Considerations

- A great way to get in-the-moment with the participants, and an alternative to on-site observational approaches.

- Provides a simple way to see the real environment as your participant experiences it, potentially noticing things that they do not think to mention. For example, how battered the product is, what else is used along with the product, the setting it is used in.

- Captures tone of voice, which can add a lot to the written comments people make, communicating the strength and direction of their emotional response. A combination of video capture with Q+A follow-up can be very insightful, as the participants help you deconstruct their own behavior.

- Consider whether you are just looking to capture video from the respondent in any setting (like a video interview), or if you want mobile video for out-of-home situations?

- Are your target participants likely to have video capabilities in their mobile device, and know how to use them? Or will you need to help them learn?

- For a participant to share a video requires a significant degree of trust in the researcher. You will want to consider how you will build that trust, and move from less challenging and less personal to more challenging and more personal assignments.

· · · · · ·

MINI CASE STUDY: Bank machines

A bank wanted to look for innovation opportunities with bank machines. A discussion forum with video assignments was used over a three-week period. The discussions occurred first, and included capturing of ATM experiences. A subset of the discussion participants was invited to participate in a second, video phase of the project. Video participants were of all ages, representing a very broad cross-section of society, including a woman in her eighties, a young mother with small children, and a mid-career male who traveled a lot in his work, stopping in different communities. The online discussion was excellent, but the video footage really brought the project to life. The young mother made a passionate case for the importance of drive-through machines, complete with visuals.

One challenge people had was a worry about looking either weird or criminal, and holding the camera while using a bank machine was clearly a problem. Participants sometimes kept talking while they put the camera down, or provided a recap immediately before and after their transaction. We also had some wonderful footage in their homes, including one cat that was a real camera-hog!

➲ **PRO TIPS:** Provide clear assignments to capture mini-movies including the activities of interest. Encourage participants to keep their video clips short, or you will find yourself stretched to watch all the footage. Have a plan to manage the footage, and be sure to provide clear disclosure about how the video will be used.

Mobile

Mobile has really been trying to break into the city of insights for years. We remember early Blackberry users trying to participate in discussion forums on their handhelds, long before the average citizen had mobile internet capabilities. Today, mobile capabilities are so mainstream that new possibilities have opened up for getting into the world of our participants.

Mobile platforms are available, but mobile should really be looked at as an access point, not a methodology.

Mobile App or Mobile Browser?

Some platforms now exist that are exclusively mobile and are constructed as a stand-alone application, or app, with no expectation or possibility of logging in without it. Constructed as a stand-alone app, they are designed to capture short text responses, photos or video.

Other platforms are like a bus with multiple doors. You can enter through the app door, or enter through the internet door, either on your mobile device or on a computer or tablet.

Another difference between mobile platforms is the ability to capture mobile input in the absence of an internet connection (with the data later uploaded when a connection is present). Some apps can do this, whereas others cannot. Depending on your location and your target audience, this may or may not be an issue, but it is certainly worth considering at the design and recruiting stage. When participants are on restrictive cell phone plans, they may not want to use their bandwidth allowance to upload a video when out of the house, and prefer to wait and upload via Wi-Fi in a café or plugged-in to a desktop at home.

Newer handhelds provide the interesting option of dictating a response, which is then converted to text, potentially permitting longer answers than people typically type on a handheld device.

Some platforms provide the opportunity to push questions or reminders to the participants through various means, including a notification in the app itself, a text message or an email message.

Mobile offers the wonderful possibility of bringing online qualitative to populations that have traditionally been difficult and expensive to research. For much of the world, internet access and computing generally will continue to be dominated by wireless and lightweight devices such as handhelds and tablets. As developers become increasingly skilled at translating device capabilities to research usage, we are likely to see a continued stream of innovative possibilities for virtual observation. Today, mobile is often discussed as a methodology. But the pervasive expansion of mobile access means it will soon be just a different doorway.

Considerations

- Mobile excels at getting in the moment, immediate actions with your target audience; where they are, right now. Instead of getting reactions hours or days later, you are looking at a lag time of minutes between the activity of interest and the impression.

- Mobile access means easy capture and upload of photos and videos, so it can be very convenient for the participants even if they are in their homes or workplaces. There is no need to transfer the photos or video from one machine to another for uploading, for example.

- You must take device capabilities into account at the design and recruiting stage if you wish to rely on mobile. Is your target likely to have a device and be comfortable using it? Increasingly, the answer to this question will be yes, but not always.

- Device compatibility will continue to be a consideration, with legacy mobile operating systems not always fully compatible with leading edge platforms.

- Privacy considerations become increasingly important when non-participants may be captured in photos and video. We discuss these considerations further in Chapter 6.

- The mobile device "knows" where it is if connected to any kind of mobile network. Geo-location capture and tracking is a bonus for researchers, but does present another privacy consideration that must be disclosed and managed.

· · · · · ·

MINI CASE STUDIES
Dogs on video

The objective of the project was to identify new product and service opportunities with dog owners in major markets around the world. Participants used a mobile app to capture photos and video for a week and at different times of the day in an individual diary. Then participants were brought together in each country to discuss overall themes in a threaded group discussion. The final phase of the study provided the participant groups with basic training in creative thinking followed by idea generation.

Mobile access permitted abundant photo and video capture in the moment that took us into the participants' world during mealtimes, play-times, walking, sleeping, and even bad-dog moments. While some participants chose to use a larger screen (desktop, laptop, or tablet) for easier keyboarding of the group discussions, others focused primarily on mobile as their input device. Larger screens appear to support more in-depth commentary, and make it easier for participants to navigate a detailed discussion. However, the handheld device is always handy, a strength for entering into the world of the participant anytime and anywhere. The combination of the two can provide the best of both worlds.

The hybrid approach of mobile self-ethnography via the diary, and in-depth group discussions using a threaded discussion was powerful, producing a tremendous amount of data, and identifying numerous opportunities for category innovation. While recruiting for smart-phone use can be a source of sample bias in developing markets such as India and South Africa, as time goes by, mobile approaches may become more inclusive than other methods.

· · · · · ·

Nutrition on the move

To test a new concept for a nutrition app, participants with "poor nutrition habits" were recruited to participate in a three-phase research study that began with collecting individual responses in the moment and ended with testing the usability of the nutrition app on participants' mobile devices. (In between these two activities we had a group chat.) For the first phase of the study, 400 participants were contacted via their mobile device randomly once a day at self-selected mealtimes (through email and/or SMS text, depending on their preference). Participants were asked to respond with a picture and description of what they were eating and why, and the nutrition grade they felt they had achieved with the meal. Those who completed the intercepts were invited to participate in the chat group. Nearly 200 participants who attended the chat group were invited to download a beta version of the client's nutrition app. Those who downloaded the app and registered were taken to a short survey about their eating habits. After one week, participants were surveyed again about their eating habits and their review of the new app.

Extended Community

Throughout the online qualitative landscape you will find the word community attached to so many approaches that you might well be confused about what is meant. The word is so evocative that it has now been applied to everything from a three-day discussion forum to a multi-year extended engagement. Platform providers talk about "community platforms" as if this is a special technology. If you ask a dozen QRCs to define what a community is in qualitative terms, you are likely to get more than a dozen definitions. Even the names can be confusing: Marketing Research Online Community (MROC), Marketplace community, Insight community.

We are not saying we are right on this, but here's our view:

A community is an extended research engagement with a group of participants that have been screened and recruited to the research project in some fashion. We like the term Insight Community, but it's the same thing as an MROC. (Marketing Research Online Community.) The purpose of this type of community is to gather insights from the participants.

A marketplace community may look very similar on the face of things, but there are a couple of key differences. A marketplace community is about influencing opinion and generating brand loyalty, even if insight is on the agenda. Participants in a marketplace community are generally not screened; they just join the tour.

In our view, an insight community is not a technology; it is a way of engaging with a target group of participants over an extended period. The technology is an enabler of this, but the engagement can take many forms, just as when you look at how people can arrive at a cafe. It's like seeing a really nice highway coach rolling into town – the ones where the outside is as polished as a kitchen appliance – and you just know the inside looks like first class seating on a trans-Atlantic flight. Some people get off the bus, while a few may arrive in a mini-van, others come by scooter, and still others may arrive on foot!

Think of a community as an extended project where there is a home base. That home base is likely (but not necessarily) going to be some kind of online platform that has extended-time threaded discussion capabilities at the core.

Once you have a home base, you can add on any number of ways of interacting in real time or extended time, and even face-to-face.

Unlike most qualitative research, an extended community is not an ad-hoc project designed to address a limited set of objectives. Yes, there should be clear objectives, but they are likely to be considerably broader (involving multiple or relatively complex products goods or services, for example) and deeper (looking for longer-term opportunities as well as immediate tactical feedback). An important dimension is also extending the duration of engagement with the participants. Are you able to capitalize on watching behavior and attitudes over an extended period with the same group of people?

Different client organizations use extended communities in many ways. If they are large enough, they can provide quick-hit, mini-quantitative support for fast turnaround questions like tactical promotions, almost like an access panel. However, as the number of participants in a community grows, it will indeed look and act more like an access panel, where the participants do not necessarily know each other, and the weekly time commitment is measured in minutes, not hours.

Our interest in communities tends to lean more towards going deeper with extended insights, using the tools of qualitative to gain new levels of understanding that can be used to drive innovation and competitive advantage and understand the customer (or user, or patient, or consumer) journey and experience in a holistic way.

Consider the difference in participant experience between the two possibilities shown in the table on the next page. These are just two possibilities, and you can design a community engagement in many ways. There is no one best way.

Considerations

- Keeping people engaged over a longer period of time is a major consideration. You want enough to discuss that no one gets bored and drifts off. How will you use the opportunity to obtain deep insights into the lives, attitudes, and behaviors of a group of participants?
- Managing the amount of data obtained, and socializing the insights into the sponsoring client's organization will require significant planning.

	Extended community A	Extended community B
Number of participants	5,000	50
Weekly time commitment, on average, over several months	5 to 10 minutes, optional response to invitations to participate in a specific activity	30 minutes a week, with a combination of required and optional activities
Moderator role	Friendly familiar face that posts activities and encourages participation.	Individual engagement with follow-up questions and continual rapport development.
Interaction types	Mini-polls, markup of visual images, open ended comments, threaded discussions.	Some simple activities, some requiring in depth journaling or discussion. Occasional invitations to real time activities, such as online focus groups.
Recruited how	Online recruiting and screening.	Telephone screening by a qualitative recruiter using standard screening methodologies.
Incentives	Points and contests combined with intangible motivations (fun, engaging activities, sense of contributing to positive change).	Cash honoraria at regular intervals, supplemented with contests and intangible motivations (fun, engaging activities, sense of contributing, feedback on impact of prior contributions).

Now that we have made this case, you will notice that we are referring to online communities through much of this book. It just seems simpler, and many of the platform providers for long term and ad hoc short term extended studies are the same. When someone uses the word "community," you are well advised to seek clarity about what is actually being discussed.

· · · · · ·

MINI CASE STUDY: Year-long forum

A vitamin supplier sought to understand how people attempt to improve their own health and nutrition. Twelve hundred pre-screened physically active vitamin consumers were invited to join a year-long ethnography study that included a variety of group and individual activities using chat, mobile intercepts, diaries, forums, and in-store interviews. Panel members were told they could be invited to participate in a total of up to 5 hours of research activities at the rate of $100/hour within one year. Panel members were invited to complete at least two 10-minute online surveys for $10 each. Segments of the panel were given specific activities to complete, including weekly diaries, product reviews, photo boards, chat discussions, ad markups, and store visits. For each activity, panel members were segmented by gender and age, as well as attitude and behavior, which were variable over time. The entire panel was surveyed online after each of two media campaigns were released. Reports were provided after each activity, and quarterly client meetings fueled changes in direction to marketing and product development strategies.

CHAPTER 4

Objectives, Methods & Tools

[Where to go, how to get there and what to pack]

Mapping Your Way

Now that you have determined your mode of research transportation, be it boards, chats, or some other combination of online methods, it's time to map out your journey. We'll look at ways you can get around, roads you can take, and various destinations of interest.

In the big city of insights, there are many places to visit and explore. The most popular spots are those that benefit from the anonymity and geographic reach online affords.

Before conceiving your study proposal, interview your client about the research objective, participant requirements, and recruiting options. If your client comes to you "to test some ads," dig a little deeper so you can design the most effective plan to get there:

- How did the need to test the ads come to be?
- What stage is the advertising development?
- In what format will the ads be tested?
- Exactly how many ad versions will you need to test?
- What key questions are being asked within the organization?
- How will the results from your analysis ultimately be used?

As a QRC this kind of questioning is right up your alley. Seek out the critical clues from your client to design the most effective online qualitative research study. The list that follows is by no means comprehensive, but it does represent the wide variety of the places you can go with online qualitative research:

- Advertising and message tests
- Brand discovery
- Brand image and positioning research
- Concept tests and new product development
- Customer experience plus satisfaction
- Establishment of consumer vocabulary for questionnaire development
- Ethnography
- Ideation and brainstorming
- Name and logo tests
- Package design
- Website usability

Mapping the city of insights is an ongoing effort. Possibilities continue to pop into existence as technology advances our capabilities and expands the experience. Before you start packing, figure out what route you're going to take to arrive at your research objective. There are many roads leading into the city, so begin by asking yourself these four questions:

1. What are you testing?
- New concept?
- New design?
- New product or service?
- Print ads?
- Promotional materials?
- Sales communication?
- Websites?
- Videos?

2. What do you need to know?
- Design feedback?
- Usability?
- Brand Positioning?
- Awareness?
- Recommendations?
- Behavior?
- Attitudes?
- Language?

3. How will the results be used?

- Short-term decision making?
- Long-term decision making or planning?
- Part of a larger study?
- Ongoing research?
- To confirm or dismiss earlier results?

4. How will the results be presented?

- By whom?
- For whom?
- How?
- Where?
- Part of a larger initiative?

What to Pack

Once you have a clear understanding of where you're going and why, now you can start packing. You're in charge of everyone's baggage for this trip, so think about what you need (or want) on the journey. What will make the trip faster? Less expensive? More comfortable? Not only will you need things for the journey, you'll also want to pack the things you'll need when you arrive at your destination. There are more tools available than you will need, so consider your mode of travel, budget, schedule, and desired outcome before making a platform selection.

Each destination (research objective) is different and requires a different set of tools to make the experience worthwhile. Some tools will be part of the platform (think seats and tires), and others you may want to have simply because they will enhance your trip (like a radio or GPS). Consider what you'll be doing and the experience you want everyone to have. Is the trip relaxing or filled with activities? Will you be camping or staying in a hotel? Ignore these questions and you'll be ill-prepared to succeed at reaching your intended destination.

As you can imagine, there are many different routes from which you can choose to get to your final destination. Thankfully there are a number of tools designed to help you navigate whichever roads you choose. Let's look at some different online qualitative research tools and discuss what they do and how you might use them.

Branding

Some platforms give you the option to brand the communications you send out or the facility itself. When participants receive the push notifications from the platform, will they be "from" you (also called "white label"), or will the platform company's name be noted (a la "powered by TechCo")? When participants and clients enter the virtual facility, will they see your company logo, or the platform's logo? Consider the impression you want to make and the information you want to reveal to participants and clients when deciding how to brand the experience. There may be a charge for custom branding, so be sure to ask up front if you require a particular setup.

Moderator mode (text, image, audio, video)

As the moderator, how will you present yourself to participants? Will you be on a live video feed? Will you have a pre-recorded message for participants to hear? Will you welcome them by typing text? The method in which you choose to communicate with participants online is determined by how you want participants to receive your information. For example, if you are interviewing a group of mechanical engineers about a complex new drafting tool, you may opt to describe the tool in a video, either live or recorded, so your participants can hear you describe its features while simultaneously pointing them out on the tool. If you're interviewing young adults about a television show they watch, you may decide to communicate your questions via type while showing them clips in the whiteboard because you want collective input in real time and need the flexibility to go "off guide" at the spur of the moment. Think about your questions and how your delivery will give the participants the opportunity to communicate their responses effectively. It'll also be wise to take budget and project deadlines into consideration, as different modes of communication require different setups.

Push communications (email, SMS, MMS)

One of the necessary features in the vehicle you choose on your journey will be push communications to your invited participants. Sending messages via email, SMS (Short Messaging Service) or MMS (Multimedia Messaging Service) or some other means is critical to maintaining participant interest and ensuring a smooth trip. You'll be communicating instructions, facility links, and reminders to participants, and possibly even invited observers before and during your study. Having SMS or MMS capability, in addition to email, can be helpful when dealing with younger audiences or those who simply prefer to use one means over the other. SMS and MMS communications also open up a larger range of mobile possibilities.

Some platforms will allow you to pre-load messages and reminders, which can be helpful when organizing multiple discussions or with larger communities. Some platforms will let you create and re-use communication templates. Others will allow you to completely customize the content. Basic capabilities are essential, but on larger and longer projects, you may benefit from more flexibility, like being able to send out automatic reminders when a new activity goes live.

Administrative tools

Most likely your platform will come with some administrative controls to which you will have access during data collection. During the discussion, administrative tools may enable you to send private messages, dismiss or ban (remove or block a participant), or even edit participant posts, or other actions. Other tools may include the ability to put participants into sub-groups, invite select participants to virtual break-out rooms, hide the group conversation from participants, require questions before proceeding, etc. A full tour of the platform you'll be using will help you better understand what capabilities you, and possibly your assistant, will have during the actual interviews.

Participant response mode (text, image, audio, video)

Whichever platform you're using to reach your objective, participants will be able to respond to you in some fashion. Consider whether you want responses all at once, or over an extended period of time. Do you need participants to respond to your questions with typed responses? Audio? A recorded video? A live webcam feed? Think about your questions and what mode will give the participant the opportunity to communicate responses effectively, and provide you the contextual information you want.

If you are testing advertising, you may also want to consider how much control you need over the duration of exposure to the stimulus. In real time scenarios, you can control this. In extended scenarios, you may not be able to have this control. Choose your platform accordingly.

Participant tools and activities

Platforms also offer different ways for participants to respond and interact with the moderator, as well as other participants. Some tools that may be included can enable marking-up images and documents, creating poll questions, making collages, and creating breakout rooms on the fly, among other features. These accessories may or may not benefit your study, so check to make sure you're only paying for what you want.

There are almost always multiple ways to handle any given need. For example, you can ask people to mark up a concept, or you can ask them just to comment on it in text form. Both are effective and both are equally valid. Another example might be doing a photo projective activity. In person, you might lay down a stack of images and ask everyone to pick two. Online, you could get a sophisticated photo-sorting tool designed to do this, where people click and drag images into their responses. Or you can just show people a set of labeled images and ask them to choose the letters corresponding to the photos that reflect their ideas about the topic before elaborating.

Back to our transportation analogy, you really do need wheels on the ground and gas in the engine to move your research vehicle forward. But while computer-aided parallel parking may be a nice luxury to have, it is not essential to getting the job done.

Activity tracking

When participants respond to your question or request, you need some way to know. Especially important in extended time group studies, look for platforms that will give you lots of information for keeping responses on-schedule and organized. For example, does the platform allow you to see a summary of an individual participant's responses by question over time, or only collective responses by question? When a participant submits an activity, where does it go?

If a participant drops out of a real time chat, how will you know? As technology advances, geo-location tracking via mobile devices will be another feature you can use. When it comes to activity tracking in online qual, the key is not the volume of information provided, but the ease in which that information can be understood. Ask the provider for a screen shot or picture of activity tracking to be sure it will be useful for your specific needs.

Observer input and experience

Like the back room in a traditional focus facility, most online qual platforms have an observer channel of communication. It may be in a separate area, or integrated into the discussion, but observer comments are always private and never visible to participants. How much of the conversation does your client need or want to see? What screener data about each participant is visible to observers during the discussion? While clients will vary in their level of involvement in the research, you'll want to look for a platform that will allow them to communicate as much, or as little, as they want.

Alerts

Especially in extended-time studies, receiving alerts when a participant or observer has added to the conversation can be extremely helpful. Alerts are push notifications that come from the platform to you, notifying you that an activity in your board discussion has occurred. Some platforms will give you the opportunity to customize what triggers your alerts and how often you are notified.

Pre-loaded elements

For every online qual study you will have some form of discussion guide and most likely one or more visual stimuli. Most platforms allow you to pre-load your discussion guide questions and stimuli, as well as set the parameters and resulting action for participant responses. Look for real-time platforms that will allow you to upload your discussion guide questions in advance of the live chat, but also allow you to type free hand so you can probe participant comments effectively. Some platforms will have a slide creator within the platform, allowing you to customize slides that are preformatted to fit within the platform. If the platform doesn't have a slide creator, it will most likely have a feature allowing you to upload files you can use as visual stimuli. Be sure to follow the formatting requirements for the platform and test everything in the platform in advance of the group to ensure it can be viewed consistently across different operating systems, browsers, and devices.

Transcripts

Transcripts are the text of your interviews. In any text-based online qualitative study, the platform will provide you a log of the discussion. In video-based online qual studies the "transcript" is technically a video file. In addition to the participant responses, ask the provider what else, if anything, is included in the transcripts (private messages, observer comments, moderator notes, stimuli presented, etc.). How are graphic activities captured and reported (e.g., individual and collective heatmaps, annotated docs, etc.)? Transcripts are typically provided in a format you can work with, either a basic text file (with extensions like txt, csv, rtf) or a familiar document extension (e.g., doc, pdf, xls.)

Activities given to participants are also logged, so be sure to ask how you track and view those elements. If participants submit collages, for example, how do you access those files for your report? If participants evaluate a particular stimuli, what reports, if any, result (e.g., heatmaps, click-tracking, etc.)? Some extended-time platforms display a progress meter for participant activities, which can be helpful in extended group studies when monitoring multiple assignments.

Analysis features

Some platforms have features designed to help you analyze the results. These can be both helpful and distracting. Tools like text analyzers, sentiment scrapers, and word clouds may be available in the platform you choose. If you already have a system for analyzing transcripts with which you are comfortable, you can always continue with what works for you by simply exporting the raw transcript from the platform. If the platform has features that save you time and get you a little closer to your analysis faster, then by all means have at it! Some analysis tools, however, can be time-consuming and will take you away from seeing the big picture. Not to discourage you from trying new tools, just know that not all bells and whistles features are useful for every study.

One feature that can be especially helpful is the ability to flag or tag participant comments. Either on the fly, or in the transcript, being able to identify a set of comments in a single swoop can save an enormous amount of time when you're moderating multiple discussions.

Provisioning [shopping for tools]

Beyond a map (research design), what else do you need to have with you? You may choose to work with a provider who has all the tools you need, or you may choose to do-it-yourself (DIY). However you proceed, beware of tour guides trying to sell you a map to the stars.

The number of possible tools continues to grow. Even though they have similarities, learning a new platform does take time. If you have a tech-geek gene, you may enjoy continued experimenting. Or, you may want to choose a couple, get comfortable with them, and stay with them. It is often easier to think about the design of a project once you are familiar with a platform. When your client asks, "Can we do this...?" you will be able to tap into a good answer. These days, that answer is almost always going to be yes, because the tools are simply amazing. In your own head, you will be pondering which of the tools that you know well will best handle the task at hand.

Then there are more prosaic concerns, like technology compatibility and data security. This might all feel a bit daunting. Keep in mind that there are almost as many details to running in-person events that are equally baffling to the newcomer. If your project is straightforward and short term, you can probably use any platform to get the job done.

Questions to ask the provider

Here's a list of questions that might guide your own investigation. At one time or another, we have enquired about all of these topics.

Overview of the platform
- What was it designed to do? Ad hoc research or extended community?
- What size of groups can be created? Is there a recommended size? Why those parameters?

- Can participants of one group participate in another group? Can they do this with a single log-in ID?

Pricing and access

- What is the basic pricing structure?
- How long do I have access to the platform outside the time that the project is live? If my schedule changes, is there a cost for this?

Pricing structures in the industry have varied a lot over time, and are likely to keep evolving. Some of the approaches you are likely to encounter include fees that increase as the time and number of participants on the project increases. Flat pricing may also be available from some providers. And subscription models allow you to have much greater access to the platform, for months or years, for a one-time or re-occurring fee. Some platforms charge for additional moderator access, and others do not. Platforms vary in the amount of time you have access before and after your project is live to participants. Some archive all projects indefinitely and others charge for continued access. Not only should providers answer your questions, they should also offer you a free trial before you commit, so be sure to ask.

Technology compatibility

- How do participants gain access to the platform?
- If access is intended to be mobile, is it through a mobile browser or through an app? What mobile operating systems are compatible? What platforms was the app designed for? Will the app work if there is no internet connection, i.e. can videos be recorded and uploaded later? Can text questions be answered when offline?
- If access is expected to be via a browser, what is the oldest version of the major internet browsers that can access the platform successfully?
- Is any kind of a download required on a computer to participate?
- Are there any other hardware or software capabilities that must be present for the platform – or for specific question types – to work correctly?

Oddly enough, we have found that browser compatibility is more often an issue in B2B research projects than in consumer projects, if the browser is to be used at the workplace. Large organizations may "lock down" the computers of employees, so that no changes can be made to the software, including any kind of download required to enable some web meeting platforms. They may also be using quite dated browsers. With their own computers, people can choose to simply download a more up-to-date browser. If your B2B participants can use their own equipment, this isn't an issue. However, if you want them to participate from the workplace, you will need to consider this aspect, as well as any firewalls the business may have in place that could potentially block the platform's website.

Unfortunately some platform providers may be reluctant to be up front about these details. Keep in mind that you may need to include requirements in your recruiting specs, so push for understanding. For a global project, you will need to consider the incidence and penetration of smart devices and internet access. If an app will only accept input when there is a wireless internet (WIFI) connection open, this may (or may not) be an issue for your project.

Maintenance and backup

Platform providers are getting more sophisticated with their handling of software updates, but how they manage maintenance and back-up is still worth checking. It can be very disruptive to you and your participants if things change mid-project.

- How are updates to the platform handled? Is there anything scheduled to happen during the window of your project?
- How often are backups done?
- Where (what country) are servers located?
- Is the project on a dedicated server or a shared server?

Backups are more for your own peace of mind. We have, by mistake, deleted things from our project we did not want to delete, and were very happy to find out that the platform was able to restore the information from its backup. If you and your client invest in a long-term community, you want to be sure that some unexpected disruption is not going to wipe out valuable data.

Some clients care about the country location of servers, and may even include requirements of this kind in your services agreement. This is more often a concern if they are providing you with a list than if you are using recruiter sourced participants. The provider may be able to offer you a workaround if this becomes a problem.

Some platforms put all client projects on a shared server. Others use dedicated servers for each project. This might seem like a crazy thing to care about. However some clients will ask about this for privacy and security reasons. From your standpoint as a moderator, if your projects are not on the same server, you cannot easily move things between projects. If you are doing a lot of online work on the same platform, it can be handy to quickly and easily go into a previous project to copy questions, or even a whole discussion guide that you then amend.

Security

- What security measures are in place to protect your data, your customer list, and so forth?
- What security is used to ensure the platform itself is not compromised?

Your topic may not be top secret, and your clients may not be worried about data security, but it is an element of online qual in which you should be well versed and knowledgeable. Professional platform providers are likely to have pretty good answers to questions about data security. If you are using open source tools or DIY tools such as a social network, you should give data security some serious thought. Most clients do care about the privacy and security of their proprietary research data and many will assume your recommendation includes fundamental security measures.

Conducting your studies on a secure server, or a website that requires a login and password to access, may be critical to your study and your client. Especially if your research is proprietary, make sure your platform offers the means for you to keep the data private and secure, both during data collection as well as after the study is completed.

Stability and tech support

Asking a technology provider which things don't work well is a bit like asking your surgeon how many of their patients have died recently. It's awkward to ask and hard to get a straight answer. You might try phrasing along the lines of "Are there any features participants seem to have difficulties with?" "What are the top five reasons people call tech support?" "What things are buggy or just don't work well, sometimes on short notice?" "What kind of tech support is available and what hours and days does it operate?" "What kind of response time could I or a participant expect if we contacted you with a problem?"

In practice, it is helpful to ask other researchers about their experiences.

Tech support can be important. A problem with a live online qual study can very quickly feel like a crisis. The problem may well have been one you created yourself, because you failed to flip the "on" switch and no one can see your topics! Trust us, this is the voice of experience speaking here. Problems that participants are having will quickly fall to you if there is no tech support. And truly, what are you going to do to troubleshoot their problems? If it is a real time project, you absolutely do not have the time to troubleshoot for a participant. Some platforms offer support via phone, others want the initial request to come via email. Whichever method, be sure you know the drill and are satisfied with the turnaround time.

Most marketing research is not happening on a business hours schedule. We are all grateful for those platform providers who either deliver something that just always works, and for those that will respond to our panicked email at almost any hour of the day or night. They have our thanks, and our loyalty, even if we don't say it often enough.

Project support

If you need time to learn a new platform, your provider may offer several different kinds of support. Some offer personalized training, moderator forums, or regular webinars. Others will walk through your project before it goes live to help you identify any issues or glitches. Some have help tools in the platform to explain setup. Others have how-to videos. Before choosing a platform provider, consider their training method, experience and availability, and fee, if applicable.

You should also know what kind of support services are available as part of the basic rental package e.g., uploading of participants; what additional services are available and at what cost; what kind of training is provided on the platform?

We have suggested, elsewhere in this book, that there are times you may want more support on the actual project. If you are swamped with work, you may want help uploading the guide, for example. It is helpful to know what kind of support is available, and how these services are charged.

Basic capabilities

- What tools are available on the platform? (See the tools section above.)
- What types of question formats are available?
- What types of responses are possible?
- What is the cost of a basic rental?
- Are there any additional charges for service or support?
- Can you do it yourself, or does the platform have to be set up by the provider?

Online platforms have become a fairly feature-rich environment, a trend that is likely to continue. There may be some features that cannot be set up on a DIY basis. There's nothing wrong with that, as long as you know the time and cost involved. Platform providers often have good ideas and creative ways to do things, if they understand your objective.

Profile information

- What kind of profile parameters can you attach to a participant?
- Can you segment on these parameters within the platform?
- Do participants use their own name or is an anonymous name assigned?
- Can participants upload their own photo or choose from a set of avatars?
- Can participants add to their own profile information?

Visible profile information of participants can be very helpful to both you and your observers during an online qual study. Observers should never see personally identifiable information (PII) about participants.

Platforms do vary in terms of how they handle profile information. Some require you to input it, perhaps via upload of your recruiting grid. Others will let you put some of this work onto the participant, by letting you ask profiling questions that they answer, either free-form or multiple choice, just like a questionnaire. With extended time studies, it can be helpful to have participant photos or avatars, as these will let you very quickly scan to see who is answering what, and these also add to the visual appeal of the environment.

Segmenting capabilities

Being able to segment your data based on participant profile information can be a big time saver, especially with long or complex studies, as you can easily direct specific questions to certain people, and the like. Some extended-time platforms offer the ability to segment participants into sub-groups during the discussion. There is more variability among platforms in this area than you might guess. If segmentation is going to be important, make sure you understand exactly how it works.

- What segmenting capabilities does the platform provide?
- How can the segments be used? e.g., push communication, directing to questions, for data analysis?
- What kinds of segment parameters are possible?
- Can transcripts be filtered by segment?

Transcripts and deliverables

- What are all the ways and formats a transcript can be downloaded?
- In what ways can transcripts be filtered?
- How are multi-media responses handled?

After you gather reams of data – and you WILL get reams of data – you need to be able to get it out of the platform. Transcripts themselves are a relatively straightforward matter, and most platforms will give you multiple options for viewing and download, e.g., filtered by single participant, in spreadsheet format, or as an HTML file.

When it comes to photos, videos, and visual markups, you have a different story with a lot of variations. A one-week online visual diary project with a dozen participants can easily generate hundreds of photos and dozens of videos. Be sure you know what is involved in getting your multi-media data out of the platform. Are you clicking and saving each file? Are there possibilities for bulk downloads? Or would you rather leave the output on the platform and just use it there? In that case, make sure you know what your archiving situation and costs are.

Capacity and limitations

- What are the limits of . . . _____?
- I'm thinking about doing . . . does that give you any concerns at all?

Your concern might be the size of photos, the number of participants, the length of videos, or something else. Most limitations you encounter can be managed, but only if you know what they are. Limitations in file size are not much of a problem anymore, but there are still limits. Sometimes a question format that is available via the browser is not available via the mobile app.

Asking questions about capacity up front will save you from discovering limits part-way through a project. If you are working with a space agency to capture user feedback from astronauts that will be relayed via geosynchronous satellite, it's a good idea to find out if there are likely to be any hiccups in the process before you launch. Okay, that's crazy, but you see what we mean. This is one case where it is easier to ask first than apologize (to the client) later.

Flexibility

- Tell me some of the different kinds of ways people have used your platform?
- If I need something a little different, what would be involved?
- What languages can be used with this platform?

If you are working in languages other than English, you will be pleased to learn that many platforms are available in multiple languages. This could include only the administrative interface and controls (e.g., "Reply" button), or it could also include multi-lingual participant responses. If you need to communicate in languages that do not use the Roman alphabet, such as traditional Chinese, be sure to ask your platform provider.

One thing to watch out for: If you are using one account for a global project, and using native language moderators in the various countries, be sure to set up your project so that a change in one group's language does not suddenly appear in all the other groups. If you aren't laughing by now, you should be, because we've had this happen!

In terms of other kinds of flexibility, here are a few things you might care about. You might want to give observers the ability to make visible posts in an extended discussion or an online focus group, for example, even if only temporarily. Perhaps you want to them to do an expert Q+A about a new service concept, then you will shut their visibility down and continue to moderate. Another thing you might want to do is let participants start their own threaded discussions or chats in an extended community. If you have a pretty good idea of what you want to do in your project, you can find out what is possible by asking a few simple questions. Providers may even offer custom solutions, the very best of flexibility!

User experience

- How does it look from the participant or client observer point of view?
- How easy is it to get around?
- How does it look in general? What's the vibe – inviting? Formal? Informal?
- What do push communications look like?

User experience is important to the success of your project. Every problem or barrier your participants encounter is less time spent telling you everything you want to know. A platform that is visually engaging and easy to use makes people want to keep clicking, and makes your work easier. Keep in mind that a more complex environment takes time for participants to learn, and may not be well suited to a short-term project. On the other hand, this kind of environment may offer more possibilities for engagement in a longer-term situation.

You will be using the push communications capability quite a bit to send out reminders, to thank people for their participation, or to let them know the schedule. In a longer project, you are likely to be answering questions or comments from participants as well.

Some extended-discussion platforms have "home pages" that you can customize a bit, by posting a video or a message for everyone. Personalized messages can convey style and tone, while also helping you establish rapport with participants. *"Today we're going to be doing something a little different – we have some new ideas we'd like your reaction to. I think you'll find this interesting."*

The look and feel of platforms is something that varies a lot. Some will let you customize the look a bit, with wallpaper or preferred font; others will not. We recommend considering your target audience when choosing a platform, as the participant's understanding and ease-of-engagement is always most important.

Extra features
- What other features are available?
- And how are people using these features?

Geo-tagging responses is something relatively new to online mobile research, and offers some interesting possibilities. On-board Analytics tools are developing rapidly – everything from tagging and highlighting to on-board video editing. Whiz-bang widgets are coming along all the time as platforms compete for your business and respond to requests from other researchers.

Like shopping for a bicycle, it is a good idea to have a clear fix on your actual needs. If you really just need a street bicycle to pedal around on and pick up a few groceries, the lightweight carbon fibre frame might be a bit excessive.

Emergency Preparedness

Before you load up your vehicle and head down the path to your destination, there's one last thing you want to anticipate: disaster. The best way to keep disaster at bay is to plan for it. You're going to need flares on-hand to help you manage an online qual nightmare. Natural disasters could include a downed server, loss of internet connection, or even an electrical blackout. Personal disasters can be even more interruptive. We'll spare you the horror stories and leave you with this:

- Notify your platform provider when you plan to conduct your online sessions.
- Login with 2 different devices when you moderate live, ideally on different internet connections.
- Train your group administrator what to do if things go wrong or if you need to leave unexpectedly.
- Have participant and client phone numbers on-hand during the live study.
- Inform participants what they should do if they lose their connection.
- Alert participants to the intended plan should the discussion shut down.

- Inform your client you are prepared in the event of an emergency. This also acknowledges that yes, there *could* be an emergency!

In addition to preparing participants, clients observing should also know what to expect. Prep your client with a clear understanding of what she will experience, including what she will be able to see and do, her role and responsibility during the online discussion (if any), and what your deliverable will look like. Like participants, giving a literal tour of the online platform to your client in advance will help eliminate confusion and give you both peace of mind throughout the online qualitative study. It is devastating to learn a confused client cannot access the platform just as you are beginning to moderate a live chat!

TRAVEL TIP   Website Usability

Website usability testing has traditionally been conducted in-person, via PC monitors and a hovering moderator on-site. Conducting usability online offers some unique opportunities for research. The journey to website usability includes identifying how customers really interact with the website, specifically: the overall appeal of the site and its contents, ease-of-navigation, how well the content of the site matches visitors' needs, the meaningfulness and clarity of the information provided, the usefulness of site features, motivations for coming and returning to the site, and recommendations for improvement.

There are many ways you can accomplish a website usability study online. Picking the best route will depend on your client's budget, schedule, and final deliverable needs. For this example, we're going to look at two possible routes that get you to the same destination: real-time individual interviews and real-time group chat.

Let's assume your client wants to understand the areas on the website visitors find most useful and why. Obviously participants need to be able to see and interact with the live website, so we're going to look for a platform that has (or can accommodate) either screen sharing or an interactive whiteboard. It also needs to be appropriate for both individual interviews as well as group chats.

Real-time IDIs

Real-time in-depth interviews will include a series of one-on-one discussions conducted on a private and secure web-sharing platform. The moderator and participant will hear each other's audio, and the participant shares his screen with the moderator. The moderator sees the participant's mouse movements and hears self-reported descriptions from the participant of what he is thinking and doing on his screen. The moderator can verbally request the participant to click on a link or try a particular feature on the website, all while seeing what the participant is doing on his screen.

The most important accessory you'll want to consider for this study is a real-time screen recorder that captures both the movements on the screen and also the phone conference audio. Participants will call into the conference line at a scheduled date and time, where the moderator greets them and asks a series of questions about the website. Observers receive a copy of the interview video file after the session is over, along with your topline analysis.

Real-time group chat

For a journey that involves group chat you'll want to find a platform that has an interactive whiteboard for you to push the live website to the group and have each participant individually browse the site on their own, without being affected by others doing the same thing. The moderator pushes select pages to the whiteboard for review and discussion, and directs participants to click and try features on the site, all while asking them premeditated questions about their experience. Your client receives a transcript of the group conversation and a topline report with screenshots to help highlight the insights.

For either scenario, accessories could easily be added to our study, like poll questions for prioritizing features and content, online scavenger hunts to test navigation, competitive website reviews for comparison, and click-tracking with heatmap reports showing the areas of least and most interest.

. . . . . .

MINI CASE STUDIES
Print ad test for a tourism campaign

A marketing company was consulting for the tourism board of a popular US city and sought reactions from non-business visitors to the existing print ad campaign, as well as reactions to three new print campaign concepts.

For this study prospective vacationers were recruited from an online research panel via email invitation and screened using an online questionnaire. Two online focus groups (text chat) were held in one evening and the marketing consultant and members of the tourism board observed the conversation remotely.

During the groups the moderator probed for participant feedback on three different print advertising campaigns, plus a new print ad concept. Print ads within each campaign were displayed individually on the whiteboard, then together as one campaign.

The marketing team was able to identify emotional triggers from the transcripts and develop a cohesive visual presentation strategy to attract more visitors and promote the city's attractions effectively.

. . . . . .

Concept test for a new cleaning product

An enterprising start-up company was preparing to launch a new "green" cleaning product to commercial markets. They had developed a website to support their marketing objectives and wanted reactions from purchase decision makers on the site content and features, as well as their preferred purchase method. Participants were screened via phone using a professional recruiter who purchased a list of the desired target in select industries.

Two 90-minute online focus groups were held in one evening and participants were paid for their time. During the group, live web pages of the client site were displayed to all and the moderator asked questions and probed responses. Each participant was able to navigate the website and report on desired features and content. The client team observed the group conversation remotely from their home internet connections. After the groups the client modified the sales strategy and plans to develop more specific content for the site based on concerns expressed by participants. Additional online focus groups were conducted after the product launched to obtain qualitative feedback from new users that guided the development of a highly successful marketing campaign.

· · · · · ·

Name test for a new business

An international telecom company needed to quickly gauge customer reactions to proposed names for a new small business website. For this study participants were recruited from an opt-in email list of employees at small businesses to an online screening questionnaire. In less than a week, four online focus groups were held, segmented by company size.

During the groups, participants were shown concepts for the new site and asked to comment on proposed names, which were displayed individually on the whiteboard during the discussion. Reactions were probed to determine what each name implied to participants. Mock-ups of the proposed site were shown so participants could react to the features offered. After looking at the site mock-ups, participants were again shown potential names and asked about the reason for their choices.

The client and its ad agency team observed the groups remotely and chatted among themselves online without being visible to participants. The data gathered were used to select the name of the new website, which launched shortly thereafter.

CHAPTER 5

Ethical Considerations

[Play nice with the passengers and avoid the potholes]

All marketing research should be conducted in accordance with established ethical standards as espoused by professional organizations such as ESOMAR. Chapter finished, right?

Well, not so fast, actually. As our technology gets cooler and cooler, our standards need to keep up. The city of insights is constantly under construction, and it is surprisingly easy to drop a wheel into a pothole you didn't see coming. This chapter is really about giving you some tips and checklists to ensure you stay on the right side of the dotted line.

Online research removes just about all geographic limitations to conducting research, which means you can easily be organizing a project outside your jurisdiction, where you are familiar with the laws and common business practices. It isn't really okay to say that you are complying in your own country, the one where your chair, your monitor, and your Wi-Fi router reside. You actually need to comply with the rules where your participants are. Is this strictly required by law? Who knows, and really – unless you are a lawyer or a compliance specialist – do you really want to spend your time on this, when you could be uncovering cool insights? Probably not.

Rules of the Road

Privacy laws around the world call for varying degrees of control over data you collect, and disclosure related to that data. The safest action is to keep all your project data on a dedicated, secure server and encrypt project data or shred it after returning all client-owned data. If there is any doubt in your mind at all, check in with a colleague who lives in the jurisdiction.

ESOMAR is not the only organization that publishes guidelines and codes of conduct, but the good news is, that global organizations like ESOMAR and the International Chamber of Commerce (ICC) are gradually bringing all the standards in line, and adopting consistent guidelines. For the most part, following the ethical guidelines of ESOMAR will put you well ahead of the legal requirements, so it is just a good practice to refresh your memory on these from time to time, available right on its website (www.esomar.org).

The advent of social media research and passive data collection technologies has created the need for a whole new set of guidelines.

Mobile technologies have also put the researcher – literally – in the pocket of the participant. With such intimate access, we need to take extra care, and new guidelines exist to help the researcher using these methods. We are going to touch on these topics, but not repeat all the guidelines, okay?

The Biggest Potholes: Disclosure and Consent

We always want to tell people what we are up to in qualitative research, and how the data will be used. How is this different from what you might be doing online?

Video

If you are gathering video, this is likely going to be much more personal than the focus group room fixed camera. You are getting video of people flossing their teeth, cleaning their toilet, rinsing out their frilly underwear, and hollering at their kids to shut the door. It's personal, it's close-up, and it's often very high quality, valuable data.

The video may well have others in the frame. There might be family members who are not part of the project captured in the home. There may be friends headed out for a night of partying captured in the frame of your participant's video camera in your alcohol study. And there may be perfect strangers in the café your participant sits in to do the webcam interview. Your enthusiastic participant may actually start interviewing other people without being asked, helping you find even better insights! Yes, indeed, all of these events can and do happen!

For the most part, these other people are innocent bystanders who were not recruited, did not hear the disclosure, did not consent, and may not even be aware of the research. You want to be careful about losing control over this type of footage. It's all well and good to say that you did not disclose their names, but a voice and a video can still provide definitive identification of an individual. If you doubt that this is the case, try playing the who's-that-in-the-voiceover game when you watch television advertising. You'll be surprised at how often you can identify an actor just by his or her voice.

The essential rule is: any information collected as part of your project that can be used to identify a person has to be de-identified before you release it to clients unless you have explicit prior consent.

You will also want to consider whether it is really appropriate to share intimate video with other participants during the group, or if some topics are better handled in a one-to-one mode with only you and the participant. Keep in mind that you cannot totally prevent anyone from capturing something on a screen, even a video, so just be keen to look and take the necessary steps.

Getting consent

When you are in a focus group facility, getting consent is easy. Participants simply sign a release when they arrive at the location.

With online qual, your recruiter may be removed from this step. Your platform may or may not have a customizable consent form built-in, so remember to organize consent as part of your pre-launch checklist. Consent can be obtained at the time of screening or any time up to the start of the interview. Whether consent is best acquired in-person, by mail, over-the-phone or electronically, will depend on your audience, interview method, and topic. It's a very easy step to forget when you have a lot of other things to manage.

Passive data collection

Many platforms you can use will collect passive data for you, such as geo-location or IP address. Other technologies can track web-browsing behavior. This can be really helpful, but the participant may not know you are collecting this information. You want to be sure that this tacit information is not being inadvertently disclosed to other participants.

Is the App Playing Nice?

If you are asking your participants to download an app, make sure it is also playing nice with their devices. It shouldn't change any settings (certainly not without telling them) and shouldn't be secretly capturing other data (like what other software is on the device, for example). Don't assume that your technology supplier has a background in research or understands ethical practices.

It's also a good idea to ensure that the research app is reasonably user-friendly, for you and the participants. Just as the user experience varies with different online platforms, the app experience should enable great feedback, not leave users feeling frustrated with the technology.

Anything the participant has downloaded and installed should be easily uninstalled once the project is complete.

Children

Research with children always requires extra care. You will want to follow the guidelines for your country in terms of the definition of a minor, because it is different from place to place. In the United States, websites that are collecting information from children under the age of 13 are required to comply with the federal Children's Online Privacy Protection Act (COPPA). Established in April, 2000, the rules spell out what a website operator must include in a privacy policy, when and how to seek verifiable consent from a parent or guardian, and what your responsibilities are to protect children's privacy and safety online.

Any research conducted with minors should include parental notification, understanding, and approval of what data will be collected and how it will be used.

One great thing about online qualitative research is that the children can actually be in the safest, friendliest place – their own home, with their own parent or guardian nearby. Be clear in your planning just who is supposed to be participating if there is any potential for doubt. We don't want Mom doing the homework! If you are using a design where there is going to be shared participation, e.g., parent and child, set up separate log-ins or otherwise plan how you will separate the data.

Once the Project Starts

You still have a few ethical potholes to deal with once the project starts. Some of them are more likely to happen in an extended project, when participants have more opportunities to get to know the others in the group.

Enthusiastic over-sharing

First, participants may reveal their identities despite your guidance. For business participants, it is just second nature for people to say who they are and where they work, even if you have been diligently trying to keep this information from being disclosed to your client observers. In extended discussions, you can edit out anything that shouldn't be seen, and even send a private note to explain why.

Another challenge, mentioned earlier in this chapter, is the participant who is trying to be helpful by collecting views from others and bringing them into the research. You've done such a great job at building rapport that people want to help you, and they start videoing their friends and neighbors. Be clear in your pre-group instructions, and this should not happen. If it does, contact the participant directly and explain why you can't accept these generous contributions, no matter how well intended.

The longer a project goes on, the less likely it is that people will remember that this is a research project, and the more likely they will feel connected to the group. We rely on this as part of our engagement strategy. However, it is your responsibility to keep all the passengers on the bus safe until the tour is over.

Requests to connect

The longer a project goes on, the more likely it is that two participants will want to connect with each other directly. You really don't want to be responsible for anything nasty that might happen as a result, so don't encourage or enable sharing of personal contact data. If you do decide to let research participants connect on their own, ask them to defer it until the end of the project.

Occasionally you will find that participants want to connect with you, especially via social media. Good for you. This means you did a great job moderating! But be cautious about letting this happen. You have a special relationship of authority to anyone in a research project, and should be extremely cautious about entering into a continuing relationship on any level. Best to explain the need for you to maintain your role as the researcher and decline. Keep in mind that old adage, "decide in haste; repent at leisure."

Anonymity

Being able to promise genuine anonymity is a real advantage of online research. If there are no pictures or video, and only first or fake assigned names are disclosed, people should feel safe to say practically anything. Participants have little to no anonymity if they show their face on a webcam or in a shared picture or video. Depending on your study objective, offering participants complete anonymity can result in extremely candid feedback on personal and sensitive subjects.

Small markets

Small markets present a special challenge for anonymity, even online. This could mean a small market because of sheer population size, for example. But it can also be a small population in terms of your research. For example, senior medical specialists are likely to know each other even if they live in different cities. The smaller the target community you are engaging, the more likely there will be a personal connection that you didn't anticipate.

In one financial project we conducted, a participant in one city asked to withdraw because she recognized a participant from another city and was not comfortable being in the study with him. We explored the situation, and finished her participation in a phone interview.

When People Argue on the Bus

You need to manage any hostility or negative comments with extra care when you are not in-person. In the middle of an in-person discussion, you will know right away if someone has stepped over the line in their comment to another participant, and can manage that situation immediately. Sometimes, in text, it is harder to tell, particularly if the norms of the group are very different from your own, e.g., big age difference. You may think it is friendly disagreement, and discover later that someone was offended.

You have to sleep sometime. On extended projects, this means comments will be posted potentially for hours before you see them. Under these circumstances, it is simple logistics, not nuance, that becomes the challenge.

If in doubt, use escalating tactics to manage the situation, just as you would in-person:

1. Set clear ground rules at the start. Disagreement is great, but it has to be respectful and civilized.
2. Remind if necessary that it's okay to disagree, but there can be no food fights.
3. Privately ask the offending party to tone it down.
4. Privately ask the person you think may have been offended if they are okay, or whether you should step in.
5. Edit or delete anything problematic.
6. Shift the difficult individual to a one-on-one discussion with you, removing them from the group.

If you are deliberately arranging a controlled conflict situation, such as a debate, be prepared to manage it, just as you would in-person. Research might feel like an intense experience for participants at times, but it should never be disrespectful or cause unhappiness.

· · · · · ·

MINI CASE STUDY: Blind online

A discussion forum project involved reviewing features of a website and commenting in the discussion. Part way into the project, a participant got in touch via email. She was blind, and was navigating everything using her computer's voice synthesizer. She had not disclosed her blindness, and had honestly expected to be able to complete the project.

A few of the visual exercises could not be done, so those were replaced with a phone interview. The client was able to get some interesting and unexpected feedback that its website was very easy to use for a blind person using basic computer aids.

Online qualitative offers the opportunity for many people to participate in research that might not otherwise, because of physical disability, location constraints, illness or other barriers.

CHAPTER 6

Calculating Costs

[What's the cost of visiting the City of Insights]

To understand costs, it's critical to first have an understanding of what your client wants to get out of the trip and the desired final deliverable. It's also nice to know your client's budget, but consider that information a luxury if you're so informed. Most likely you'll want to offer your client a range of options for the journey. The good news is that the city of insights is vast, offering a wide array of travel options, from low-budget hikes to lavish jet setting.

Once you have an idea of what the research journey will entail, think about the money and hours you will probably invest to make it all happen. Like any qual study, consider costs for:

- Participants (sourcing your Sample, designing and administering the screening questionnaire, verifying identities, and instructing invited participants)
- Facility (technology, training, and support)
- Moderator (designing the interview guide, moderating the discussions, and analyzing the results)
- Incidentals (assisted labor, transcription, stimuli setup, video hosting, interpreter, etc.)
- Final Deliverable (reporting and presenting insights)

Each of these cost areas contains elements you'll want to consider before figuring out what price you want to charge your client. Let's look at each area separately, beginning with the end.

$ Project Deliverable

Calculating costs for a study can seem overwhelming at first, so we recommend you begin with the end in mind and consider your final deliverable first. When the trip is over and you have your client's final insights ready, what does it look like exactly? Is it a written document or a slide presentation? Are you presenting the findings in-person or via the web? Will your insights have a life after the project is complete? How will the findings be used? What does your client expect to do with the results? Is this a single ad hoc project, or part of a multi-phased initiative? What scheduling dependencies exist outside of your work?

This line of questioning is right up your alley as a qually! Get in there and start probing so you can propose a trip itinerary that is well suited for your client's research needs.

Reporting

Your value as a qualitative researcher goes far beyond designing discussion guides and interviewing research participants. Imagine being in Rome and your tour guide simply dropped you off at the Coliseum with a map. The best tour guides will prepare you for the trip, make you feel comfortable, educate you throughout the experience, point out key places of interest, and answer all your questions. Whether your clients have been to the city of insights before or not, a good tour guide makes every trip unique and worthwhile.

Reporting is changing

Businesses today are under constant pressure to increase the speed of complex processes, such as product development cycles, without reducing the quality of the work. As researchers, we are now also under market pressure to re-imagine and re-invent the steps in our processes. Many of the methods discussed in this book do help the researcher greatly reduce the time needed for fieldwork. Detailed analysis and reporting can still be time-consuming, especially when other project elements are waiting. If you can explore options for different kinds of reports – for shorter reports, interactive debriefs, topline only reports, and even infographics – you may be able to tighten both the timeline and the investment.

Presenting

At the end of your trip you may be asked to present the research findings to your client, either in-person or via the web. It's best to know in advance to whom you'll be presenting, and to how many, as well as where. When figuring costs, consider travel time and expenses required to get you there and back, including equipment to present effectively, if not readily available at the location.

You may also want to consider the possibilities for presenting using a web meeting platform if travel time or expense is a barrier.

$ Research Participants

Every qualitative research study needs participants. The process of sourcing, screening, verifying, and inviting participants is nearly the same, offline or online, as are costs to recruit and incentivize participants, which obviously vary from study to study.

One key difference between online and brick-and-mortar facilities is that many online facilities do not recruit. Online facilities are often developed by tech companies who know little to nothing about marketing research recruiting standards (for more on recruiting, see Chapter 7). We strongly recommend contracting a reputable research recruiter who will verify participant identities and provide you with the PII you need.

Incentives

If your recruiter is working with his or her own database, you will typically pay a set fee per qualified individual recruited. Otherwise, your "sample" or "list" fee may be a separate charge.

When recruiting from a pool of prospective recruits, respondents typically have two incentive opportunities:

1. Reward to take the initial screening questionnaire
2. Reward for selection and full participation

Screening incentive

Large panel providers often have reward systems in place to encourage and retain members. Be sure to understand whether those costs have been accounted for in the bid, or if you need to figure what will entice prospective respondents to complete the screening questionnaire.

If you opt to include a screener incentive, you'll want to consider your audience and what will encourage them to complete the questionnaire. While providing an incentive to everyone who tries to qualify will certainly work, it will probably blow your budget before you even begin the research study. To combat this, often a sweepstakes incentive is used. With a sweepstakes, a small number of respondents are selected at random to receive a pre-determined prize after recruiting is complete. The idea is that a chance to win *something* will encourage people to proceed and see if they qualify.

Staying out of trouble

A note of caution to those looking to DIY: The rules of your sweepstakes serve as a contract between you and the respondent and should be carefully drafted by someone who is experienced and understands how to comply with the laws. Sweepstakes (also called contests, giveaways, or competitions depending on the country) are usually governed by contract law, as well as other specific laws and regulations that vary by district, and are anything but consistent. Sweepstakes are heavily regulated because of the potential for abuse and the association with gambling, and it is easy to fall afoul of the rules.

If you plan to use social media to promote the sweepstakes, you will also need to follow *their* rules. Your client may have an attorney who can consult on these matters; otherwise you'll need to hire a professional sweepstakes management agency to handle the promotion. Most online qual studies include a geographically dispersed set of participants, which necessitates the review of regulations in each jurisdiction. Over certain amounts, rules can change. To sleep well at night and avoid the risk of penalties, call the pros.

Participant incentive

Incentives offered to online qual *study participants* are usually calculated based on the value of participants' time and the expertise they bring to the table. Participants in a single group should all receive the same incentive. A basic rule of thumb, online or offline, is to consider how much your target market earns as well as how valuable their specific feedback is to the study, and offer the incentive accordingly. A high-powered real estate executive in a study about gum packaging shouldn't be paid any more than the other participants, but if the study is about high-end real estate, you're going to need to cough-up a bit more to entice your true target market to participate.

Longer durations tend to be more costly than real time, even when the same time commitment appears to be involved. For example, a 90-minute real time commitment feels like a smaller investment than 90 minutes over the course of three days in an extended project, and you may want to consider paying a bit more.

Distribution

Sending checks to participants can be costly, while payments made through online banking systems and electronic transfers can be relatively inexpensive, depending on your location. We expect to see electronic forms of payment becoming more mainstream. If you are running a global study, be sure that you can get payment to your participants in a method and currency they can use, or seek guidance from someone with more experience. Know who will be responsible for distributing incentives and be sure they are equipped with all they need to turn the payments around quickly.

Recruiting

To obtain an accurate recruiting quote you'll want to understand both the expected incidence rate (IR) and the anticipated qualifying rate (QR) of your desired target. IR refers to the percentage of the available population that can be expected to meet the initial basic screener requirements. QR refers to the percentage of those who will fully qualify for selection, not only based on all the screener requirements, but also their availability and willingness to participate.

IR for any study will vary depending on how narrow or broad the qualifying screening criteria are. If your client is looking for adults who stand upright, you could confidently estimate an incidence rate at close to 100 percent. If you need to find adults who stand upright while sleeping, your IR rate will be much, much lower. When researching an existing product or product category, your client can probably give you a good idea of what IR to expect. If not, you're going to have to guess.

QR is usually a conservative percentage and can be significantly affected by the value of the incentive to participants. If participants do not feel the incentive payment is worth it for them to talk with you, QR will decrease. For reference, an online chat with a fair to generous incentive can expect a 30 percent QR in most situations.

The important thing to remember is to include your assumptions in the proposal with your price. Not sure? Include different prices for different anticipated response levels. The recruiting price you provide your client should be qualified by both IR and QR estimates, otherwise you could end up paying out more than you bring in. If that happens to you, it probably won't happen twice!

Understanding the recruiter's quote

Recruiters often provide bids on a per-complete basis, although some may provide a flat fee for a fixed number of recruits. Others may separate the list or sample cost from the actual screening efforts. Be sure to ask what the recruiting fee includes, especially incentive costs *for prospects to complete the screener* (not to be confused with incentives for participation, described earlier in this chapter). It's also good to ask for prices for additional recruits, in case more are needed after the study gets going. Other elements that will affect cost are:

- Project timeline
- Source of potential recruits (client's customer list, a managed panel, website intercept, etc.)
- Means of recruiting (email, online intercept, telephone, direct mail, in-person intercept)
- Total number of qualified recruits to be interviewed
- Length of the screening questionnaire (time investment required by the recruiter to administer and the respondent to complete)
- Participant requirements and group segmentations
- Duration and intensity of expected participant involvement and commitment required
- Value of the incentives offered
- Means of incentivizing participants (mailed check, direct deposit, PayPal, gift card, other)
- Incentive distribution responsibilities (recruiter, researcher, sometimes client)
- Deadline for final deliverable

Recruiters will serve up those who are willing and available to participate, but rarely will they provide any guarantees as to who will actually show up for the research. If you want a cost per participant where you are not charged for no-shows, you will find the cost is correspondingly higher. On the flip side of this, there may be no charge to replace no-shows if you know ahead of time. Show rates for online qual studies are very similar to face-to-face work, meaning that you should plan to over-recruit anticipating that 10 to 20 percent of invited and confirmed recruits will not show.

	Text chat group	Three day discussion	In-person focus group
Confirmed recruit	25	18	8
Expected show rate	18 to 22	15 to 16	6 to 7
Drop out after starting study / incomplete data	Usually zero – people who show-up plan to participate	Plan for a small number: e.g., 1	Usually zero – people don't leave after they arrive
Over-recruit needed as % of required number	15 to 30%	10 to 20%	15 to 30%

The above chart reflects our experience, and your own experience may be different of course. (YMMV or "your mileage may vary"!)

Using client lists

The use of a client list, in this era of privacy concerns, can create some significant advantages and disadvantages for you. Depending on the type of project, working with a list can be more or less costly than other methods, partly dependent on the quality of the list. In a high-incidence study, a list can be invaluable. However, in a low-incidence study you'll need to reach out to more people, all of whom have not expressed an interest in participating in research. Client rules for managing these lists are becoming increasingly onerous, in terms of moving around and handling the data, particularly in financial and health-related industries. You may need to obtain privacy agreements with every subcontractor you work with. Your client may have their own internal guidelines about how often they reach out to anyone on their customer list, and will want a status report as to who was and who was not contacted.

If your study is not blind and your client can be revealed to prospective recruits, often you will experience a higher open-rate if the email invitation comes directly from your client. In those cases, simply provide your client with the screener link to include in the email they are sending. Screener links can often be customized so clicks from the email can be counted and tracked.

There is no substitute for clear communications. A good recruiting partner can make many helpful suggestions, and will likely have encountered your data security challenges before.

$ Facility and Setup
Toolbox

The key to estimating the cost of your toolbox is to know what tools you need inside, which is why we began this exercise with the end in mind. Choose tools that will be valuable on your trip and help you prepare your ultimate deliverable. If your client expects an engaging presentation with video clips of the participants responding, then you'll need a webcam, as well the ability to record and edit the interview. You can outsource or DIY, but either way there will be toolbox costs to take into account.

We talked in Chapter 4 about the different tools you can use to get the most out of your trip. The tool(s) you need may already be standard in the platform, or you may need to add accessories to maximize the results for your specific study. You'll want to figure costs associated with the platform, as well as the expense of any other tools you may be using.

For example, if you're conducting one-on-one interviews online using a screen-sharing platform, there may be a fee to use the platform and an added fee to record the session. You can expect an additional cost if you want the session transcribed. If you're running a discussion board study and need participants to do a collage, that feature may be built into the platform or you may consider using another collage making tool. Whatever the tool's feature, assume it comes with a fee unless clearly stated otherwise.

Mechanic

However you're traveling, it's always nice to have a good mechanic. In the city of insights, "mechanics," or administrators, handle the setup and maintenance of the running parts of the platform. Some DIY platforms will assume you're the mechanic and offer ad hoc help for a fee. Full-featured platforms will probably offer you a mechanic to help you set up the facility and help prepare you and your participants for the study. Your platform administrator can also provide you the transcript or recording file at the end of the session. Ask your provider about the mechanics of the platform, who will be managing the logistics, and what fees, if any, will be charged.

Driver

For complex or long online qual studies, you may want to consider hiring another qualitative researcher to share some of the heavy lifting on your journey. Coordinator, co-conspirator, assistant, project coordinator – whatever you call the position, a good driver has experience with the vehicle and may even know the back roads, giving you a chance to look around and take in the study scenery. Especially helpful with discussion boards that run for several weeks or months, a driver can help you monitor conversations and maintain a high level of input from participants. A driver can also be helpful in real-time studies, coordinating participants and homework activities, making reminder calls and assisting with any last-minute changes to the study itinerary. You won't need to hire a driver on every study, but you may want to consider having an experienced research partner riding shotgun on your first trip to the big city.

$ Moderator

Calculating your fee as the moderator can be tricky, and no two moderators are alike. Every qual researcher has unique experiences, specialties, and methods of capturing insights. Consider your distinctive talents, as well as efforts you anticipate on the following project study elements:

- Project management
- Screening questionnaire
- Recruiting
- Discussion guide and visual stimuli

- Participant coordination, communication, and support
- Client meetings and de-briefs
- Moderating the session(s), duration, and quantity
- Analysis and report

You may view these various tasks as having different levels of professional skill involved, even if you choose to do the work yourself. Administrative tasks can be time-consuming, but not high value-added relative to moderating or analysis. Another consideration is the ability to control your time. Being able to work at your own desk in your pajamas versus sleeping in another hotel room is also something to consider.

For extended projects, you may be able to moderate more than one group at a time. In our experience, two is manageable, three is quite demanding, and four is a Herculean task that will barely leave you time for basic bodily needs like eating and sleeping. You will need to decide for yourself if your studies will be value-priced (value of the work to the client) or priced based on hours you anticipate spending.

$ Incidentals

While online qual may eliminate travel from the expense line, there are some additional costs that may creep into your study. These costs are best disclosed upfront in your proposal so neither you nor your client is caught by surprise.

Devices

In certain situations you may need to physically mail your participants equipment in order for them to interact effectively (e.g., web cameras). In certain areas of the world, or even in remote parts of developed countries, you may even need to pay for access to the internet in order for the representative population to participate.

In this age of smart technology, this may seem surprising. However, the "tools of the future" are unevenly distributed – some people seem to have a lot more than others. If you do need to provide a device, you may want to consider whether it can also serve as part of the incentive value.

· · · · · ·

MINI CASE STUDY: Sending netbooks to executives

During an extended B2B project, we wanted to provide something exciting and motivating to the senior level staff in a wide variety of large corporations that would really get them keen to participate. Netbooks had only recently arrived on the technology scene, and were relatively inexpensive. We knew that cash would not go over well, and that some would not be able to accept the cash regardless, due to corporate ethics rules. The netbooks were presented as the mode of communication, not the incentive.

We carefully selected a good-looking model to send out to about 50 participants in Canada and the U.S. Our initial plan was to have all of these sent from an office supplies superstore that provided free shipping. Our order of so many computers going to multiple addresses was flagged as fraud, and our account was shut down for days while we sorted out the problem.

In the case of one major conglomerate, the netbook was very useful – the only way to get around the corporation's very secure data environment was to have them install an internet line outside the corporate firewall, which they were not prepared to connect to a desktop being used for work.

Several corporations told us they could not keep the computers, and we suggested they raffle or donate them to a local charity. We know for sure that at least five netbooks went to a Ronald McDonald house, which everyone felt happy about.

Interpreters and translators

If your online qual studies are in a language you or your client does not understand, you'll want to hire an interpreter. Translators can translate discussion guides and invitations. Interpreters perform a vital role during data collection. Extended studies in a foreign language can be aided by an interpreter, who can re-post participant comments into your native language as the study is live. Interpreters in real time studies can audibly translate the chatter live via a separate audio line connected to the moderator and client observers. The same individual may be able to both translate materials and provide live interpretation.

However, simultaneous interpretation is highly skilled and demanding work, and usually carries a correspondingly higher rate.

Keep in mind that the research is only as good as the interpreter you are using, as that is who your client will hear. Choose one with references and test the process on the platform you intend to use before the study goes live.

Transcription

If your interview is recorded in an audio or video file, you may want to have it transcribed for convenient review and analysis. It's much faster to review a 10-page summary of a one-hour interview than it is to listen to the same interview again for an hour. Plus, clients rarely have the time or interest to listen to full recorded interviews, even with video. Online qual studies using text will automatically include a log of the discussion. Instant transcript!

Report writer

Not necessarily the study driver, a report writer can be a great asset if you have a lot of data to sort through. A report writer with a fresh perspective can sometimes offer insight you may not have seen.

$ Overall value

Once you have your cost estimates lined up, you will want to weigh overall value of your alternative approaches against the value of the insights to the client. Your best option may be a hybrid approach, where you use some methods to obtain richness and give the client a better feel for the customer (e.g., video interview) and another online method to fill in gaps in the data.

Consider another possibility as well – that you will want to take a few participants from a group session and do an in-depth interview with them. You have many options for adding enhanced value even after the study starts, without the logistics associated with, for instance, multi-city facility bookings.

The one thing you generally do not need to provide for is catering. No one has yet invented the virtual sandwich tray. Or the virtual backroom goodies, which is really a shame, since we imagine they'd be deliciously calorie neutral.

CHAPTER 7

Recruiting to Online Qual Studies

[Finding the right people to invite
to your research event]

Plan the Event

Now that you have toured the city of insights and considered places of interest, it's time to decide who to invite!

Your target audience will vary by the type of event you're organizing and the type of event will depend on the capability and availability of your target audience. Be considerate of your prospective guests and plan an event in which they will feel most comfortable. (See Chapter 4 on the different online qual methods available.)

Compile the Guest List

If you do not have available access to a sample source from which to recruit, there are outside panel companies, opt-in email lists, and customer databases you can consider. You may even want to recruit from multiple sample sources.

Most research recruiters, including brick-and-mortar focus facilities, have panels (or panel partners) that go beyond their own geographic boundaries. For online recruiter recommendations, reach out to your colleagues for referrals, or begin your search with trusted industry associations and their respective directories.

Each recruiter has competencies in different markets, as well as different identity verification and reward methods. If your market segment has low incidence, consider recruiting to your online focus group by phone, direct mail, or even in-person.

Don't be fooled into thinking online studies require an online recruit. Choose the professional recruiting method that will most effectively identify and screen your desired target audience. The critical question is whether the prospective participants have access to the internet at the designated day(s) and time(s).

Statistics for World Internet Use

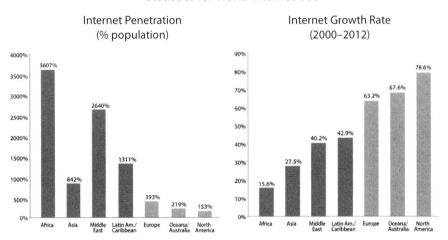

Source: internetworldstats.com

Most people in popular target markets today have access to some form of internet connection. Markets with lower access are rapidly catching up, as the table showing global growth rates illustrates. Even folks with a dial-up connection can effectively respond using text-based methods online.. In many developing markets, access to an internet-connected mobile phone is more common than computer-based access.

In the U.S. statistics show very little difference in internet usage between men and women, and among White, African-American, and Hispanic groups. Usage is very high across all age groups under 65, and more than half of those over 65 are regularly connected. Internet usage rises with education and income levels. Urban, suburban, and rural areas are all well over 80 percent in penetration.

One common misconception about online studies is that the participants can easily be impostors, making the data collected invalid. Much like phone interviews, participant identities can be validated and confirmed by hiring a well-respected and trusted recruiter. Thanks to a team at ESOMAR, we can all be smart buyers of research sample. Helpful publications specifically related to online research recruiting can be found on the ESOMAR website.

In addition to being online, consider what equipment or devices will be required for respondents to participate. Will they need a webcam? A smart phone? Any mobile device? What about operating systems? Studies can easily be biased if only users of a particular device or system can respond, unless, of course, that's what you're testing! The ability to confirm a participant's qualifications is critical and best managed by professional research recruiters. Like trying to shoot a gnat with a shotgun, searching for qualified recruits via online panels or list companies can be more expensive than recruiting through traditional recruiting methods.

To obtain an accurate recruiting quote for an online qual event, be prepared to divulge the following:

- Interview method and duration
- Project start date
- Participant time investment and the incentive offered
- Total number of participants, requirements, and group segmentations (if any)
- Incentives (amount, method/type, and responsibility of distribution)
- What you want the recruiter to handle (sample only, online screener, incentives, etc.)
- Technology requirements of participants
- Other necessities for your specific study

Be sure to establish with the provider exactly what data you need to collect, as it will most certainly include personally identifiable information (PII), such as name, phone number and email address. Sounds obvious, but not all online recruiters are familiar with qualitative research and won't assume you need this critical info. And list companies are even less helpful in this area, since even those willing to share PII may not have the person's consent to do so.

Some professional recruiters work only with research clients on the dark side (i.e., quantitative), who only need the numbers. These providers have policies in place that actually prevent them from giving you any PII, designed to protect their panel members, and their proprietary panels. Additionally, some online recruiters may require that you use their online platforms to collect the data, which may or may not be what you want), so just be sure to ask those important questions up-front before leaning in for the kiss.

Watch the Weather

The city of insights can be brought to a standstill when Bad Sample rolls in. If you purchase a bulk email address list, if your client has a list with no confirmable source, or if the list you have contains only email addresses, it's time to hunker down for the impending storm.

When planning your research event, don't let bad weather play a role. A good professional recruiter is like event insurance, supplying you with tents and all the supplies for making your guests comfortable. And just like insurance, you are well advised to shop around and ask lots of questions before signing the agreement. And if the bids you receive vary widely, it may be an indication that your recruiting requirements were misunderstood.

Save the Date

Once you have a prospective guest list, it's time to determine who is qualified and available to attend the research event.

Whether you are recruiting on your own, or working with a provider to locate prospects for you, you'll want to design an unbiased screening questionnaire. The fundamentals of the screener will be the same regardless of the recruiting method. If you're recruiting by phone or in-person for an online study, be sure to screen for available internet connection, and any other technological requirements not identifiable by phone, like computer speakers, microphone, or a webcam, for example. Over the phone, be sure to confirm the participant's email address, as email is most likely how you will communicate with your study participants. An incorrect email address is a pretty big barrier, so best to double-confirm proper spelling.

Pre-qualifying participants for some level of "online communication skills" is up to you, as it will depend on who you are interviewing and the objective of the study. If needed or requested by the client, consider adding an open-ended question or two at the end of your screener that requires a thoughtful text response, either on or off the study topic, to provide more insight for final selection. Taking a look at respondent email addresses can also be quite revealing, as surveysformoney@email.com should probably be left at the door.

If you decide your online study merits an online recruit, you'll want to choose an effective platform to administer the screening questionnaire (one that monitors or doesn't allow the respondent to change answers). Often the recruiter or facility provider you choose will handle the online screener administration as part of their service. DIY survey programs are also an option, just be sure to test your survey and the resulting data before going live. No matter how careful you are, programming mistakes are inevitable. To prevent errors from ruining your study, triple-check your survey codes and run test data to ensure results are coming through as you intended.

If you opt to hire a professional, online screener programming costs will vary depending on the number of questions and the number of respondents. Some recruiters will require that they use their screening tool with their panel, so be sure to clarify what options will be available, especially if you want the option to DIY.

TRAVEL TIP   DIY recruiting

You can design your own screening questionnaire using an online survey tool. Some great do-it-yourself survey tools exist online for free, with low costs for added features. They're relatively simple to learn and enable you to gather screener data and manage recruiting on your own.

DIY survey tools are handy when you already have an email address list of people you need to screen further. A big advantage of setting up your own online screeners is that once you have a template, you need only modify it for future studies.

- Include a Privacy Statement so respondents know what data is being collected and how it will be used.
- Name your survey something unrelated to your client or the research topic so as not to reveal segments or the client's name (the survey name may appear in the survey URL).

- Include questions that cover standard industry screening and excludes "professional respondents."
- Include questions for email address and phone number.
- Include a response deadline in your invitation, in addition to the URL link and incentive rules.
- If you are recruiting children to participate in research online, be sure to comply with the rules. In the U.S., the Children's Online Privacy Protection Act (www.coppa.org) applies. Globally, ESOMAR is a good place to start.
- To catch people who appropriately disqualify, remember to include hidden questions in your survey programming that will identify those who do not qualify, that way respondents who go back to a page and change their answers in an attempt to qualify remain tagged and can ultimately be removed from consideration.
- Identify which screener questions, if any, have some flexibility in the responses and opt to tacitly tag those respondents instead of disqualifying them immediately. When reviewing your screener results be sure to acknowledge those tags and make your selections appropriately.
- Throughout your online recruiting, keep a keen eye on responses. Assuming all the email invitations have been sent out, you should have most of the groups filled after two full days. By the end of the third day you should feel confident that you can fill all the groups completely. If you have any concerns, act quickly to enhance recruiting and ensure fulfillment.

Another bit of advice for pioneering DIYers: You may need some additional skills to prevent your participant profiles from looking like a scrapbook when you hand the goods over to your client. If you want snazzy looking documents like the better recruiters provide, and you're not into learning a bit of graphic design, outsourcing to a report writer or someone skilled to add flair can keep your deliverables looking professional.

In addition to the survey tool, to DIY you'll need a sample source, as well as a method of inviting prospects to your online screener. If your sample sources are limited, remember you're only as good as your first attempt and bulk email blasts have never seen a high response rate. For the best results, consider using a service or program that specializes in sending custom emails and knows how to get through SPAM filters. Not to discourage the adventurous from giving it a try, just proceed wisely and consider having a backup recruiting option.

While a reputable recruiter will always confirm participant identities, be sure to follow-through with this critical step if you decide to DIY. The ESOMAR documents are a great resource and offer basic online recruiting standards even DIYers should follow. Since qualitative research utilizes a smaller sample base than quantitative surveys, a reliable list verifying service can often be cost prohibitive. Fortunately or unfortunately, a quick search online today can offer a world of information about a prospective participant. Whether your study is B2B or B2C, social media and reference websites are steaming with publicly available information that can quickly confirm or deny a participant's age, location, phone number, and more. Whether you ask participants to recall demographic information for confirmation, or seek data online to corroborate their qualifications, verifications should be made before official invitations are sent.

The Big Event

You'll want to invite enough guests to your event to create the desired interaction, but not so many that the party gets too crowded and out of your control.

Situations do vary, so consider all factors (incentive amount, participant relationships, etc.) that may affect show rates before deciding how many people to actually invite. For example, some experienced online moderators can manage up to 18 or 20 participants at a time in a text environment, while others prefer smaller groups. We strongly recommend that if you are new to online moderating, consider inviting fewer people to each group, or hiring a backup moderator to attend your groups for support.

Speaking to participants before the online study is highly recommended, as the outreach is known to consistently raise show rates. Regardless if you actually recruit by phone, reach out and give each invited participant a call before the interview. Some recruiters provide outreach by phone as a follow-up, or you can make the calls yourself.

Connecting with participants on a more personal level than just email dramatically increases their interest in the study and their confidence in you.

Invited participants can be a little skeptical about an online research study, despite having gone through the screening process. Hearing your voice secures the relationship and assures each participant that you are real and interested in hearing his or her opinion in the online study. The phone call is also a great opportunity for participants to ask questions and for you to confirm receipt of your emailed instructions. If needed, you can guide the participant through the online platform you'll be using to address any functional issues in advance of your online discussion.

· · · · · ·

MINI CASE STUDIES: Recruiting to text chat groups

A popular online retailer wanted customers to provide feedback on its marketing plan for a new e-reader. Participants were recruited from an email address list of their customers who had previously expressed interest in sharing their opinions. The incentive for participating in the 90-minute chat discussion was generously set at $100 each. Invited recruits were contacted by phone on the day of the group to confirm receipt of the instructions and to coordinate the correct start time in their time zone. Out of 25 pre-qualified and invited customers, 24 showed up to participate. Three were asked to leave due to over-crowding, but received the full incentive.

The Debrief: We probably could have considered a lower incentive, but the client was thrilled with the high show rate.

· · · · · ·

A well-known car manufacturer sought feedback from prospective customers on the print advertising campaign for a new luxury automobile. Participants were re-cruited from an email address list of sales leads provided by the company. The list contained only email addresses and names. No other information was available. More than 4,000 emails were sent to find 25 respondents who qualified for par-ticipation. The incentive for participation was set at $100 each. Instructions were sent via email and reminders were sent via email instead of made by phone to save time. Out of 25 invited recruits, 6 showed up to participate and 4 completed the full 90-minute discussion.

The Debrief: The client wouldn't budge on the incentive. Knowing we had a low incentive for the desired target segment and a poor list should have prompted us to over-recruit and secure alternates, as well as make phone calls to invited recruits days before the event in order to utilize the alternates effectively.

Emerging Recruiting Methods

Recruiting is a target area for innovative ideas, as many organizations seek ways to leverage the power of social media and other new technologies to streamline and speed up the recruiting process. At leading industry conferences, often there are any number of organizations showcasing a new recruiting approach. These are exciting developments, and we expect that ultimately there will be many new ways to bring guests into the city of insights.

Whichever recruiting approach you choose, the key is not to lose sight of land – the basic considerations described in this section. Talking to the wrong people, no matter how fast, inexpensive, or seriously cool the recruiting method may be, will not give you insight into your research challenge. Don't be afraid to ask some tough questions about the approach before climbing aboard a new vessel. Ultimately, you as the researcher, not the recruiter, are responsible for the quality of the work.

CHAPTER 8

Managing Online Qual Studies

[That's you with the clipboard at the front of the bus]

Getting Your Travelers Organized

There are two kinds of people in the world that love checklists – those that are naturally inclined to be organized, and those that aren't. We're part of the second camp. We don't create checklists because we love them for their own beauty, but more because we hate finding ourselves at our destination without our essentials. Over the years, we have lost computer cables in overhead bins, left smartphones in taxicabs, and almost missed our plane while picking up sparkly things in the gift shop.

In the world of online qual, it's easy to forget that you wanted to modify the graphics for the mothers-with-toddlers segment. It's easy to get distracted by your email while waiting for the next interview to start, only to be shocked out of your sneakers when the phone rings and it's the live video platform operator asking if you are still planning to dial in.

People new to qualitative research are often seduced by the moments of live fieldwork, and don't realize that there is a large amount of preparation that happens before, and an equally large amount of analysis and data wrangling that happens after that fun part. You, gentle reader, know better. You probably have a really great checklist (possibly in your head only) of things to organize for face-to-face research. Like catering, for example, something that does not come up a lot in online!

The Insights Process

This chapter is about some of the things to consider in managing your on-line study. It's organized into chunks:

- Things to consider at the planning stage
- Organizing your stimuli
- Tips to increase show rates
- Planning for administrative support if needed
- Tips for organizing your projects
- Dealing with incentives

Sometimes, real time and extended discussions are almost the same, and sometimes they are different. We'll highlight the key elements where they are different.

This won't cover every detail, but it will have enough that you can do your own creative problem solving as needed. After all, you are a researcher; problem solving is in your DNA!

Things to Consider at the Planning Stage

A few key tasks	Real Time		Real Time Extended	
	OLFG / Text chat	Web meeting interview or group	Web video interview or group	Discussion forum or community
Plan number of groups + number of participants per group	✓	✓	✓	✓
Select and arrange for a platform	✓	✓	✓	✓
Load confirmed recruits into platform				✓
Provide participant contact information to platform operator if they are handling conference call setup, or tech checks or instructions (not always necessary)		✓	✓	
Send out confirmation email with login details	✓	✓	✓	✓
Send out confirmation email with audio call-in details (or arrange to call out)		✓	✓	
Setup observers with login or call-in details	✓	✓	✓	✓
Disclosure and consent covered some-where? Participant releases if needed.	✓	✓	✓	✓

A few key tasks	Real Time	Real Time Extended		
	OLFG / Text chat	Web meeting interview or group	Web video interview or group	Discussion forum or community
Design and load guide into platform	✓			✓
Create all stimuli and test on platform	✓	✓	✓	✓
Plan how you will rotate presentation of multiple stimuli for different groups or individuals	✓	✓	✓	✓
Dry run on the platform	✓	✓	✓	
Test your AV equipment		✓	✓	
Review platform communication functions (e.g., email)	✓	✓	✓	✓
Setup administrator and review role	✓	✓		
Review conference call operator role (if using operator)		✓	✓	

Organizing Stimuli

In face-to-face environments, if you can see something or print it out, you can probably use it as stimuli. Video in-person can be tricky at times, because you have to manage a video monitor instead of a computer monitor, or possibly even have both available. And you always have access to pen and paper exercises or flipchart exercises that you create on the spot.

Use of multi-media stimuli is one way in which online is quite different. You must have a clear plan for your activities involving stimuli, and organize it in advance.

Images

You may be using images to test something like advertising concepts. Try to get a sample of the output from the client well in advance so you know what you are likely to receive in terms of format. Clients sometimes think they are doing you a favor by giving you a PowerPoint deck with the images inside it. This may work in a web meeting environment, but may not be ideal in other interview methods. Some image formats require that the viewer have special software or a reader installed to see it. Best to test all images in the platform before you go live.

Web meeting environments were largely created for the purpose of supporting presentations, and they handle PowerPoint very well. Our main tip here is that you may want to create multiple decks so that you can more easily rotate your image stimuli. It's a good idea to put in any "rejects" or back-ups as well, even if you don't plan to show them. You might learn something in the early interviews that makes you and the client reconsider what you should show. If the images are already in place, it's easy to zoom to the end of the deck and show them. Much easier than trying to load a new image while the clock is ticking and your interviewee is waiting! Like a good scout, it is always better to be prepared.

If you are using a whiteboard to show your image stimuli, just having a high quality image is all you need. Make sure your images are all similar in resolution and size, so that they show up well, and show up at the same size on screen. If the images are very different sizes, people may respond differently because of the size.

If you are using images in a photo sort or similar projective activity, a smaller image size may actually be an advantage. Some platforms will arrange a selection of images for you in a photo sort, and also automatically produce a thumbnail image that expands on clicking.

The key is to ensure you have your visuals in enough time that you can resolve any issues prior to needing them. A dry run on the platform will help you figure out what is working well and what isn't. If you can log in to the platform from a couple of different devices, this is a good way to double check what you are seeing.

TRAVEL TIP   Digital image resolution

Resolution is commonly measured as dots per inch (dpi), pixels per inch (ppi), or pixels per centimeter (ppcm). For printing images, you need a minimum of 300 dpi to get a nice crisp image. **This does not translate** to the on-screen environment. On screen, your image will be displayed at a size based on the pixels in the image. An image of 500 x 500 pixels will be displayed at 500 pixels wide by 500 pixels high. This image may only have 72 dpi, but that's ok.

Newer handheld devices tend to have very high resolution displays (high pixel density), even higher than a high quality desktop monitor. So even if your participants are looking at the stimuli on a phone, they should be able to see it all right.

There are really three main considerations:

- An image that is too large (pixel dimensions) to display properly
- An image that is too large (file size) to load quickly
- An image that is too small to show details

Most of the time, an image that is about 500 to 600 pixels wide will work well. Images that are larger than 800 pixels are likely to give some people problems, and may not display properly on the platform. You want your participants to be able to take in the image at one glance, not have to scroll to see it. An image that is 200kb to 500kb is a good file size to start with.

If you keep in mind that the avatar you see in many social media sites is no more than 100 pixels wide, you will see why you don't want to go below about 300 pixels. If you do, all detail will be lost.

Rather than ask your client for images of this size, it is best to get the largest files you can, and either do it yourself, or arrange for, the creation of the actual stimuli.

If this all sounds far too complicated, take heart. Rapidly improving technology is making image size and resolution much easier to manage. The platform may have tools to resize your image stimuli built right into it.

As always (did we say this before?) seek guidance from your platform provider. Many platforms will automatically shrink large images to the necessary resolution. Having a platform provider with whom you can easily communicate is really helpful.

Concepts and Documents

If your stimulus is words in a document, you likely have two options to choose from – use the stimulus as a document, or convert it to an image.

To display a document, creating a high-resolution image (e.g., JPG, GIF, PNG) of the document is your safest bet, as all devices are inherently capable of showing image files. Creating a PDF of your document may work, but viewers will need a PDF reader to view the file effectively. Some platforms may be able to display other kinds of documents on the screen. A document typically loads by clicking on a document icon or link – it is not immediately visible. Keep in mind that your participants will not be able to load a document on their screens unless they have the associated software installed. For this reason, we tend to display words or text as an image file.

If you want to use a markup tool of some kind, you'll find that most of these tools are designed to work with images.

TRAVEL TIP   Converting words to images

It is not that difficult to convert a PowerPoint slide into an image. You simply "save as" and choose an image format such as JPG or GIF or PNG. You can also do a simple screen capture to create an image from whatever is on your screen.

Now you have an image with a lot of type on it. Make sure you can actually read the type once you load the image in the platform. If you can't, go back and make it larger or bolder. It's a good idea to assume that viewing conditions are not perfect and that participants do not have perfect eyesight. You want people focusing on and responding to the idea, not using up their mental energy trying to read what it says.

Video stimuli from the client

Video stimuli work well online. If the video is already available online at a hosting site (for example, if the agency can give you a link), you can pull it in using the link alone. Easy peasy!

If you have access to a whiteboard, you can show the video there. Not all platform providers offer video hosting, even if they have a whiteboard. The simplest thing to do in this case is – you guessed it – talk to your platform provider and evaluate your options.

In the early days of online qual, you had to consider the bandwidth restrictions that your respondents might have, and keep files as small as possible so that they didn't have to wait to load. Then broadband arrived, and it didn't matter as much. Now that many of your participants will be on a mobile device, you again must consider bandwidth issues.

We're not even going to try to address the complexities of video formatting here. Suffice it to say that you want to ensure your video will load in a reasonable time, and be an appropriate size on the screen. Testing in advance is the only way to be sure. Fortunately, platform providers often have considerable expertise in this area, out of necessity, and can help you sort it all out. The magic of technology is making all of this easier!

Video stimuli you create

One of the niftiest options you have is creating your own video stimuli. You can introduce yourself in video, ask questions in video, and say thank you to people in video. The purpose of this kind of video is to keep the environment as engaging as you can make it for participants. It can reduce the text burden for those who are more auditory in orientation. And it shows that you will put yourself out there, just as you are asking them to do.

It's a good idea to rehearse just a little. Have a few key points written down. But don't worry about being too polished. A few tips:

- Either use the platform's built in video capture capabilities, or upload from your handheld video camera or smartphone. You don't need better quality than that.
- Keep it short. Aim for a minute or less.
- Put any mission critical information in text as well. *"I've posted a video here with today's instructions. The text below has all the information if you prefer to read it."*
- Do not set up the video to automatically load – you have no idea where your participant is viewing this, including at their place of work. Let them click it to play it.
- Show some personality, just as you would do in person. Even use visual aids if you wish.

Tips to Increase Show Rates

In face-to-face work, you may be blissfully unaware of the steps that the recruiter has taken to ensure people are present at your focus group. They confirm by phone, re-confirm by email, and they often re-confirm just before the event with a reminder call. In online qualitative research, some of this is now your role.

In addition to sending reminder emails, we strongly suggest that you or your group administrator place a personal call to each invited participant on the day of the online focus group or other real-time research event. Reaching out to each invited recruit with a combination of both visual email and audible request ensures the highest show rates. You will want to coordinate this with your recruiter, of course.

A phone call to participants in extended projects can also be very useful depending on the circumstances. For a longer project, it can help clarify expectations. For business people, it can put their mind at ease about any confidentiality concerns they may have.

The better your rapport building in advance of the research, the better your ultimate participation will be.

Be prepared to resend invitations to those who misplace them. There's no avoiding this possibility!

Getting and Using Support

In the face-to-face environment, moderators benefit from the often unseen presence of facility support staff and the recruiting team. In the online research environment, your platform provider may include some support services, but you may want additional help, either with set-up, or during the live project.

Help with set-up

There are many logistical elements to online, which we discuss in detail in this book. Loading the discussion or interview guide, loading stimuli, setting up participants on the platform, and so forth. You can choose to do this work yourself, or you can get help.

For larger numbers of participants, and for longer extended projects, you will find your need for support increases. Platforms generally make these services available (there may be an additional fee), but a research assistant could also help you.

If you choose to bring in your own support person, you will need to arrange for them to have moderator-level access to your project, either through their own login ID, or through yours.

A few of the things that we have asked an assistant to help us with on projects include:

- Taking a discussion guide from a document and inputting it to the platform.
- Copying a guide and uploading to multiple groups.
- Making modifications to the questions for multiple groups (e.g., slightly different questions for different segments).
- Inputting stimuli.
- Loading all participants into the groups.
- Assigning participants to groups and segments.
- Sending out emails to participants with login details and similar information.
- Confirming that participants have acknowledged receipt of login information.
- For extended time projects, checking that the "go-live" dates for questions are correct, especially if dates change after the guide is loaded.
- Confirming that participants have done any advance activity required (e.g., login and post a photo of the product to confirm qualification).

Moderating support

For real-time online focus groups, it is highly recommended that you have someone else in the room to function as the group administrator. The administrator acts as the initial host, welcoming participants and answering any questions they may have, and continues to provide valuable assistance throughout the discussion by monitoring participant responses and fielding questions from any observers in the room. The administrator's efforts ensure compliance by all participants and reduces distractions for the moderator.

Some of the things we have asked our group administrator to manage during and after the live chat are:

- Ensuring that all participants are responding to each of the moderator's questions.
- Fielding technical issues from participants.
- Putting clients at ease in the back room as they observe the discussion and clarifying any change in their requests before passing on to the moderator.
- Downloading the transcript or session log from the platform after the group.
- Downloading images from the live session for reporting purposes.
- Contacting the recruiter with a list of which invited recruits participated and should receive the incentive.

Whoever you select as your group administrator, be clear in advance what role you'd like him to play in the room while you are moderating. We recommend meeting your group administrator in the virtual facility so you both are familiar with the tools available and can determine who and how to welcome attendees, what policy to follow for late arrivals, how to let a participant go, how to work with clients in the back room, etc.

An operator or assistant can perform a similar function when you are conducting a web-enabled interview, with video or without. The assistant will ensure that your participants are ready and their camera or audio is working. They can assist you in loading stimuli, loading tools (e.g., highlighter tool, for you or the participants to use), and loading any poll questions you have created. Since the assistant is monitoring the session, you can ask for help, but often he can anticipate your needs, or see if you are having trouble with something.

For extended projects, an assistant can help you keep track of who has participated, troubleshoot any difficulties participants are having, and assist with similar activities. Platform providers are continually building better tools to help you do this, but on a larger project, it's always comforting to have someone else minding this element.

Longer and larger communities need a team

As you might expect, the larger the grouping and the longer the project, the more of this kind of support is needed. Those who run larger extended communities over several months or more and involving hundreds of people, often have a much bigger team to manage the community and also manage the client liaison. There may be a lead researcher who is responsible for overall design and outcomes of the project, and who coordinates with the client. A moderator is the individual who fields the topics in the community. And the community manager makes sure everyone is having a good time, getting paid, and so forth. The community manager may organize replacement recruiting, and the orientation of new community members.

The longer projects also will require a reporting cycle to be established, and have a calendar for creating and fielding new topics.

The management of a large extended community is really a large topic, and we are giving it a relatively cursory treatment here. If you are embarking on a project of large scope and scale, bringing an experienced researcher along for the ride is a great idea.

Tips for organizing your project
Terminology: Projects, studies, groups, segments

For most ad hoc research, a **project** will refer to a set of online focus groups, interviews or discussion forums addressing the same research objective. Most research projects will involve multiple groups. For extended projects, it is possible to run several groups simultaneously.

A **group** will refer to a specific research event. For example, a two-hour online focus group scheduled for a specific time and date. Or a three-day online discussion scheduled to start on a specific date. We have also referred to these as sessions when they happen in real time.

A **segment** will refer to a characteristic on which you can sort participants.

You may also hear the word **study** used as an alternative to project.

Things can become a bit confusing when you are talking about larger and longer extended communities. Consider an online community project involving

150 people that is expected to last a year. Within that larger set of activities, individual studies or projects will occur. Each of these projects or studies might involve multiple groups consisting of 20 people each. These groups could be extended discussions, e.g., a discussion forum, real time discussions, e.g., an online focus group, a web meeting, or any combination you can dream up.

Platforms that were designed to accommodate longer-term communities tend to assume that you are adding participants at the community level, and then will assign them to a specific study. Platforms that were designed with ad hoc projects in mind tend to assume you are adding participants to an individual project.

When designing your studies, it helps to have a sense of how the platform is organized.

Segments are pretty much what you would expect. They refer to characteristics that are common to a specific group of people. Typically, any given individual could belong to more than one segment. You may define a segment by a recruiting characteristic, such as age or geographic location, or product usage. Some platforms will let you define a segment inside the platform, based on the response to a question you pose.

Projects, Studies, Groups

Ad Hoc Research	Extended Communities
Project a set of research events	**Community Project** an ongoing set of research events
Group a specific research event	**Study** a specific research event involving some or all of the community
Segment characteristics that individuals can be sorted on	**Group** a specific research event within the study
	Segment characteristics that individuals can be sorted on

You may choose to put members of a segment together in a group for each research event. Or you may choose simply to use the segment information to separate their data for analysis purposes. Both approaches are usually possible.

All of these capabilities are designed to help the researcher manage projects in the most effective way possible. The most important thing is that you understand your platform and the terminology it uses. For example, it can be very frustrating to define a segment and then learn that you cannot direct specific emails accordingly. Many research platforms will let you manage multiple projects, each in various stages of completion.

Group sizes and durations

Deciding on the ideal number of people for your groups – whether real time or extended – is a decision you have to make relatively early, in order to manage recruiting. You will find that everyone has personal preferences in this regard, just as they do with face-to-face focus groups. Plus, here in the city of insights, the rules are made to be broken. All of these guidelines we are sharing with you here were created because someone tried something new.

For ad hoc research projects, the question is more straightforward than it is for longer-term communities.

Ad hoc research

For real-time projects, if participants are using voice, you have the same limitations as you do in a face-to-face focus group – you want one person talking at a time. So your total input from any one person is the length of the group, minus the time you as the moderator spend talking, divided by the number of people in the group. If you take up 20 minutes with your questions and probes, a 90-minute video group with 6 people will give you about 11 minutes of input from each participant.

In an online group chat, you as the moderator can use voice (think presentation mode), without disrupting the cadence of the discussion. Consider streaming live for all or part of the session if you need to provide spontaneous directions or demonstrate something to participants. You could also consider recording yourself on audio or video ahead of time and inserting that stimuli into select parts of your discussion guide, which will ensure consistent stimuli across multiple groups.

Online focus groups gather input using text, meaning everyone can "talk" at once. This gives you the potential for much more data collection within the duration of any given group. Depth of response is a factor, but you would not reduce group size for this reason. If you expect responses to be detailed, as they might be with more complex or engaging topics (e.g., chronic illness), you will want to plan your discussion guide accordingly and break down deep questions into smaller bites for respondents. In a group chat, the energy is live, collective and palpable, much different than an extended discussion on boards. Participants are highly engaged throughout the discussion, responding on average every one to two minutes to the moderator's questions. In our experience, time moves quickly for participants in group chats, as often they will linger after the group is over and continue to discuss their ideas.

For extended online discussions, you will want to consider expected detail as well as reading time. As the group size gets larger, there is more for everyone to read. With detailed responses, this reading can take up a lot of energy for the participants, who then feel they are contributing more time than they anticipated. On the other side of the equation, smaller numbers can sap the group of energy, and people can feel like they are all alone listening to the crickets chirping. This places a higher burden on the moderator to put energy in and keep people engaged.

	Number of participants	Duration
Online focus groups	10 to 22, depending on topic, population segment + moderator preference	90 minutes
Online video group	3 to 6. Some platforms will take more, but the advantages of the video image become lost. You as the moderator are in addition to this number, also taking up screen space.	60 to 75 minutes works well. 90 minutes starts to strain attention spans.
Web-enabled group	3 to 6, although some go up to 8. You cannot see the people so managing more than 8 can be challenging.	45 to 90 minutes
Online discussion forum	10 to 22 for consumer groups, for business people use 12 to 16 as a guideline.	2 days for a quick project. Three to five days is common. Longer durations need to be managed more like an extended community. Consider participant time commitment as well as duration. 1.5 to 2 hours per week for short projects is a good starting point.

Inviting observers

Only people you invite can observe your discussions.

When you are using a platform, you will enter the details for invited observers and send them an email with their unique login ID or access link. If the observers are listening in on an operator-assisted conferencing line, you will provide the operator their phone numbers, and also provide the observers a call-in number. Generally you can invite as many observers as you wish at no cost. The exception to this is when observers are participating via audio (e.g., on a conference calling line) where you may be charged per additional line connected.

Observers have a few ways to interact.

In an online focus group, the observers have their own channel where they can see the full conversation and also talk among themselves without interrupting the participant chat. Observers can send messages privately to the moderator or group administrator in real time. Observers are not able to talk with participants and vice versa.

On a web-enabled video or web-meeting platform, you may also be able to set up a chat window for the observers to use while they are listening (and watching) the interview. For audio, the observer lines are usually muted during the interview. After the participants have left, you may choose to open the observer audio lines to do a quick debrief.

For an online discussion forum or community, they can observe anything posted by participants (including video, photos, etc.) and comment on it, but participants cannot see their comments. They may also have their own area online to have discussions.

It is important for you as the researcher to be clear on how you want to receive any important information from observing clients. In real time, establish in advance whether your client requests will come directly to you, or through your group administrator. We've had success using the administrator as a buffer to the moderator, to enable the moderator to focus solely on the conversation at hand without client interruption. Should the client have a request or question for the moderator, the administrator receives the message first and can clarify the client's needs before answering or forwarding on, or possibly even answer directly, without interrupting the moderator at all. In extended groups, consider whether you will monitor all client comments, or if you prefer they coordinate through a single liaison point.

Incentives
Ad hoc projects

For either an online focus group or a discussion forum, you will have various tools in the platform to show you the level of participant interaction during the session. For each group the list of approved participants to be paid an incentive can be printed or downloaded for further processing. If the recruiting company you used agreed to handle incentives, simply send them the file. If you are managing the incentives yourself, use the list to prepare checks and distribute participant payments within a reasonable time period.

For any online qualitative research study, be sure you are clear up front with participants (and your group administrator) what your payment policy is for partial completion.

Extended projects and larger communities

As you extend a project over time, even a few weeks, you may choose to break up incentives into chunks based on completion of activities. This is similar to paying extra for an advance homework assignment in a face-to-face group.

Adding a contest from time to time can energize a group and make a dull activity more fun, or motivate some friendly competition for "most creative video" or similar activity. Even if the contest prize is an electronic gift certificate, someone needs to organize it, which is another activity you can ask an assistant to support.

At the end of an ad hoc project, it is a good practice to just confirm for everyone how and when they will be paid.

The larger and longer your community is, the more structure you will need around incentives, and the more you will be looking to the platform tools to help you manage this. Some large communities use non-cash rewards or points, others use a combination. Some have built-in tracking tools to assist in the process, so you can base incentives on the level of participation.

How to pay incentives

Your participants are likely to be widely dispersed – nationally, and even internationally. As long as they are in your own country, you will have a variety of the usual options, including mailing a check, or making some form of electronic payment or email transfer.

If participants are out of your own country, you will need to give this more thought. You might consider online banking systems (e.g., PayPal™), or a growing array of international remittance and wire services that operate in multiple currencies.

However you choose to distribute payments, be sure participants know what to expect when they commit to your project, or you may have a lot of communication about it later.

If you use an electronic gift certificate as a prize, be sure they can easily use it in their location. The actual gift certificate will not be able to cross borders in most cases – a certificate bought in the U.S. will not be usable in Canada, for example. With the aid of your credit card, it is easy to purchase a gift certificate in another country (e.g., Amazon gift certificate from Amazon.de or Amazon.co.uk.) We'll also state the obvious, that incentives should be uniform and unbiased. Cash or some form of cash equivalent is always better than a gifted item, and discourage your client from offering gifts of company products or branded items. Respondents will unknowingly bias your study as they tacitly seek to please the gifter.

CHAPTER 9

Real-Time Text Moderating Online

[Hosting a lively party]

For those with a taste for adventure, and a desire for less travel, allow us to introduce moderating in real time online. Real-time moderating online is similar to moderating in-person in that the discussion occurs on a set date and time and typically lasts no more than two hours.

Compared with moderating over an extended period of time, real-time moderating is very different. While recruiting and project preparation may be similar with both methods, real time is live, baby! Whether the online interview is with an individual or a group, real-time text is lively, in the moment, and exciting.

TRAVEL TIP   **Chat's Hidden Value**

When respondents are all responding to your typed question, they are doing it at the same time. Literally. Wherever they are, they are each reading the question and responding. Nobody has to "wait his or her turn" to reply and despite the continual chatter, nobody is interrupted. Pure heaven for a qualitative researcher! Basic focus group math does **not** apply:

Total time – ~~moderator talk time~~ = time for respondents.

Time for respondents / number of topics / ~~number of people~~ =
minutes per topic per person.

Being live means you never really know what's going to happen, despite good planning. The key to becoming a good real-time moderator is to first map where you need to go, then be prepared to take a different route almost every time.

Getting Started

As with any qualitative research study, your results are only as good as the quality of input, so recruiting the right folks for your study should be your first priority. Keep in mind that chat groups can not only accommodate more than a dozen participants in a single group, the discussion actually *benefits* from having that many people, if not more, conversing simultaneously, as the chatter is what generates the critical energy needed to liven up the party. Practice good recruiting standards when screening participants (see chapter 7). Remember to collect email addresses and phone numbers and confirm participant availability and access to the internet at the scheduled date and time.

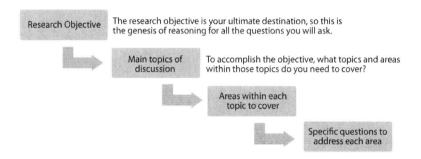

Sending Instructions

Whichever platform you use for real-time moderating, you'll want to send instructions to invited participants in advance of the discussion, preferably several days before as a courtesy, so they can confirm the date and time on their calendars, reply with any questions, and test the facility link for any issues.

Email has historically been the primary means of communication between the moderator and the recruited participant in online qual, although messaging through mobile carriers and social media channels is also possible, especially with younger participants.

Instructions should be consistently sent from the same email address. Whether part of the platform or not, keep your "from" field consistent so participants can easily recognize important notices about the study. Inconsistencies can easily land in a participant's spam or junk email folder.

Within the instructions, be sure to reiterate who you are and why you're sending the email. If you didn't do the recruiting yourself, this may be the first time the participant is receiving anything from you or your company, so introduce yourself. Sharing information about the study, as much as you can reveal, helps reiterate the importance of their contribution.

If the platform has any technical requirements, (e.g., downloaded software, certain browser types or versions required, minimum connection speed, etc.), you'll want those to be clear in your instructions as well. To keep directions short, consider using a link in the email to a page with more detailed information and troubleshooting help.

Confirming successful platform access by all invited attendees is critical to conducting a smooth real-time online study. Ask everyone to confirm successful access by completing a task in the facility, e.g., log in and send a message.

Invited observers also need to receive instructions to access the facility, so you'll want to verify before the group that all your observering clients are good to go. It's also important that your clients test the facility access from the computer they will use to view the live discussions. Success on one device does not translate to others, so be sure your clients are logged-in and comfortably settled before the group. Once the session starts, even the best of assistants will be flustered trying to deal with last minute access requests.

Reaching Out to Qualified Recruits

Reaching out to each participant before the group in a mode *other than* text is highly recommended. Reminder phone calls to each participant, or a link to a video introduction, are just two ways you can begin to establish a relationship with participants. Participants who hear and see the moderator *before* the scheduled discussion are far more likely to attend. This additional touch-point between the moderator and participants will substantially increase show rates because it:

1. Reminds participants to attend.
2. Reiterates the date and time, preferably in the participant's time zone.
3. Increases feelings of commitment.
4. Reinforces the incentive for participation.

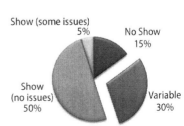

Average Participant Show Rates

Show (some issues) 5%
No Show 15%
Show (no issues) 50%
Variable 30%

Show rates are conditional, with nearly two-thirds of your invited participants at risk of becoming no-shows for reasons over which you have complete control. So what's the secret to hosting a full house and reducing lame recruits?

There are several variable factors that will affect how many recruits will actually show-up to participate in your live online study. Careful attention to each of these will ensure high show rates:

- Enticing incentive
- Clear, accurate and timely instructions
- Pre-confirmed availability
- Pre-confirmed access
- Audio or video contact by the moderator before the session
- Platform usability (compatibility and ease of use)
- Platform stability

Writing the Guide

Discussion guides for online focus groups are similar in objective to guides for in-person groups, yet different in one important way:

Questions are fleshed out and prepared with more detail, as they are usually presented to participants as written.

We've found it helpful to first prepare an outline of priorities, a logical build based on the research objectives. Then establish the desired timing for each section, working outwards from the research objective to identify sub-sections and topics we need to cover. We finish the guide draft by filling each section with unbiased questions and inserting transitional questions and instructions between topics.

Welcoming participants at the front door

Like in-person focus groups, it's important to set the tone and expectations at the start of the group. We have found that being in the chat room early as participants arrive is a great way to ease their concerns or answer any questions they may have about the facility and how they are to respond.

Welcoming participants as they enter the chat room is not only designed to make them comfortable, but also to establish the chatty atmosphere and anticipate the energy that is to come. It's also a good time to reconfirm any participant qualifications that may be in doubt, or remind participants about the study objective and the important role they are playing. Participants who arrive early to the facility are eager to engage in the research, although they may not want to be social with others ahead of time. Best to not make pre-group discussion a requirement.

We recommend starting the discussion promptly at the scheduled start time. Like in-person focus groups, your opening statement will set the tone and expectations at the start of the group. When introducing yourself to participants, you'll want to share something appealing and appropriate, and not too revealing. Anything from what you like about the rain to the last great meal you had at a restaurant, sharing yourself with the group sets an example and encourages others to open up as well.

Moderating in real time allows you to quickly set the stage for what's to come. If you have a group of kids, for example, you may want to start off with a fun video or engaging activity to catch their interest early. If you're talking with bioengineers about lab equipment, perhaps starting with a lighthearted cartoon about the industry will foster relaxation. Humor isn't always the most appropriate icebreaker, but how you welcome party-goers at the door reveals much to participants. Take the opportunity to make an appropriate entrance, one that will quickly catch their interest, not lose it.

Unlike in-person groups, real-time chat discussions specifically allow for simultaneous group input on each question. The real-time moderator does not need to "go around the room" and ask people to introduce themselves. You can initiate the introductions, then watch the responses scroll on the screen. Participants are not only answering your question, but reading other respondent answers as well.

The introduction is also good for reiterating the purpose of the research and going over any ground rules for participation, specifically how long the group will last and what's expected from participants. If the facility has any features you'll be asking participants to use, best to give them a taste early-on of what's to come, especially if it could result in incompatibility or other technical issues. You may also choose to reiterate the requirements for obtaining the honorarium, as another motivator to pay attention.

In the ground rules, be sure to ask participants to respond to each of your questions first, then react to other participant comments second. Encourage participants to respond with their first answer and not to tailor their answers based on other comments. In the real-time chat environment, the energy of the moving text is conducive to immediate answers and it takes little effort to get participants to speak their minds!

In the beginning it helps to remind participants to explain their opinions as much as possible and encourage them to share their feelings and emotions along with their written explanation. It's also a good idea to reassure their anonymity and encourage them to respond honestly and openly.

During the introductions you'll be doing most of the talking. When people respond to your introductory questions their answers will be short and without explanation. Short questions in the beginning of an online focus group are helpful for three reasons:

- Ensures all are present and responsive
- Gives the administrator a chance to count attendees
- Last-minute late arrivals can join

The platform you're using may automatically close-out latecomers, or give you the option to ask them to leave. Even if your platform has these features, be clear with your group administrator in advance exactly how many and how late people should be accepted, and what the policy is for latecomers, dropouts, and overcrowding.

In our experience, research participants are conscious of their role and are both respectful and responsive during the online focus group. Real time is a relatively fast-paced experience, forcing respondents to focus and giving them little time to stray away from the live chat. Since all participants can respond simultaneously, be prepared for a dynamic exchange of information!

Turning up the music

After the introduction you'll have a set of warm-up questions that are probably related to the topic you'll be discussing. Warm-up questions can help reveal if a participant is having trouble, which can be addressed immediately via private message or a phone call from the group administrator. You may also want to use warm-up questions to re-confirm participant qualifications, which can be cross-checked and discrepancies addressed immediately.

One of the un-sung advantages of online focus groups is the literal energy scrolling chat creates. A scrolling text conversation with 18 active participants is visually dynamic and mentally engaging for everyone involved. The key is to keep everyone talking. Thankfully, as the moderator you are well prepared for the challenge. Like any party, the group discussion takes a bit of loosening up before everyone is on the dance floor. Your first set of questions after the introductions will be your first foray into the important significant research questions. It's important for participants to understand early-on exactly what level of detail you expect in their answers. We recommend asking a question that requires a lengthy explanation first, knowing that respondents will most likely not answer the question completely. This is your opportunity as the moderator to let them know a) you are real, b) they are heard and c) you want details. Be prepared to start probing freehand every incomplete answer right away. Taking this tactic for the first couple of questions is like being the music DJ for the party. It's your job to get respondents moving! Do it well and you'll be chasing their comments for the rest of the session rather than fishing for them.

This is a short excerpt from the early minutes of a real-time online chat. Notice the short responses and continual probing, which didn't last long before responses were detailed and rich.

09:15:05	Moderator: What, if anything, would you specifically do to improve this site and why?
09:15:10	adam: I would expand the size of the student profile
09:15:12	barb: I agree.
09:15:15	Moderator: Adam, why?
09:15:17	leo: maybe use a different picture so it doesn't distract from the rest of the page
09:15:18	leslie: would move the information bar all the way to the left
09:15:20	lori: move the navigation
09:15:23	Moderator: Barb, with whom do you agree and why?
09:15:23	amy: oo i agree with adam
09:15:24	tara: i agree, addresses are important
09:15:30	Moderator: Leslie, why to the left, can you elaborate?
09:15:37	Moderator: Lori, to where would you move the nav bar?

09:15:40	lori: to the left hand side
09:15:45	Moderator: Amy, can you explain more?
09:15:48	lori: it is more intuitive
09:15:49	ted: i'd put the navigation bar to the left or at the top of the page
09:15:55	Moderator: Tara, why are addresses important?
09:15:55	barb: expanding the student profile: I think the most helpful information you can get when looking into schools is info from current students
09:15:56	terri: I don't like that the sections like in the news and upcoming events are where they are
09:16:05	Moderator: Ted, why to the left or top?
09:16:06	leslie: the address is important!
09:16:07	scott: i agree
09:16:11	Moderator: Terri, why so?
09:16:18	Moderator: Scott, can you tell me more?
09:16:20	terri: those headlines are not bolded enough...or noticeable
09:16:21	adam: I feel like the top column picture may be a little too large
09:16:30	ted: and put more info on the student/student life
09:16:31	adam: I almost thought that was the whole home page at first

Ask more, shorter questions

Because you have multiple participants responding simultaneously in a real time chat, complicated questions can be challenging for participants to answer all at once. Like being at a loud party, if you want to get participants to talk, you need to break down the questions into bite-size conversational bits. If you want to know participant reactions to a website page, for example, instead of asking what they thought, you'll want to break up what you need to know into very specific questions. Not only is this helpful to participants, but it also helps keep answers and responses to your probes on the same topic together in the transcript. Answers to a multi-part question can be difficult to analyze on the back end if participants are left to freely answer whichever parts they want. For example, if we want to know what the group thinks of a web page, we might start with this line of questioning:

- Have you visited this page before?
- What caught your attention first and what does it mean to you?
- What information on this page is most useful to you? Please explain.

- What information is NOT on this page, but it would be helpful to you as a prospective applicant?

It will be important during the live group discussion to add life to these rather stiff-sounding questions. More on how to do that soon!

Timing Your Guide

There's no guaranteed formula, but on average, figure you can get through approximately one question and the necessary probing of participant responses in about 1.5 minutes (90 seconds). You'll need to figure time for your introduction and wrap-up, as well as any topic or activity transitions. If you're used to preparing discussion guides for in-person focus groups, you will be able to get through a lot more questions online.

In general, a 90-minute online chat can cover 40-45 questions. We recommend scheduling 5 minutes at both the beginning and the end for introductions and wrap-up, as well as additional time to display (and participants to review) visual stimuli during the discussion.

Regardless how many respondents are in the room, each question will take approximately one to two minutes to complete. It may seem odd that 8 participants will take the same time as 18 participants, but the science behind real-time chat allows for just that.

In every group of participants, one will be the slowest typist and one will be the fastest typist. One will be on the fastest internet connection, another will be on the slowest. One will provide the shortest answer, another the longest. These parameters in a synchronous chat environment represent the bookends to a bell curve. The center of the bell curve is the peak of maximum responses and occurs mid-way between questions. Answers to previous questions may appear on your screen after you've sent the next question, but this rhythm is normal, and one to which you will learn to dance – from question to question, from topic to topic.

The bell curve is also a good representation of the energy flow of an online focus group. Not only does it help explain the flow and quantity of responses per question, it also reflects the flow of the actual discussion over time. As the session picks up energy, the amount of chat will increase. When designing your guide, build on questions that will excite participants. Eventually you'll have everyone dancing with abandon as if nobody's watching!

As time moves on and you pass the halfway point of the group discussion, participants will require more of your attention to stay focused. Be a good DJ and plan a few slow songs in between your rocking numbers so participants have a chance to catch their breath. Providing entertaining or engaging activities in the second half of your session will reinvigorate the crowd.

Another factor of real-time chat is the way the conversations are logged. Because the responses occur simultaneously, they are logged by the second and appear chronologically in the transcript. Because answers to prior questions may appear after the next question is sent, you want to be careful not to ask two questions in a row that could have similar answers. For example, asking "What website has the best design?" immediately followed by "Which website has the worst design?" will be challenging to decipher in the transcripts, since both answers will look similar (i.e., names of websites) and answers to the first question may flow into the conversation after you've sent the second question. This can be easily avoided by alternating question types and putting buffer questions in between ones that will generate similar looking responses. Instead of two yes/no questions in a row, for example, you would put a question in between to keep a distance in the transcript.

- What information on this page, if any, is useful to you?
  - *[BUFFER Q] For what purposes would you use the information?*
- What information on this page, if any, is not useful to you?

Although the moderated discussion does not have to follow the guide exactly, you'll most likely want to have questions prepared and uploaded in the facility so you can easily send them to the group and save yourself a lot of typing time. Having your questions pre-loaded into the discussion room allows you as the moderator to probe responses via freehand type, which saves time and keeps the conversation flowing and focused on the intended research objective. Some platforms will let you modify uploaded questions on the fly, others will not. In either scenario, consider putting encouraging and conversational comments in your guide so you don't give participants the impression you're a robotic machine. Being able to type freehand during the group is critical for this purpose.

Preparing the Facility

Either you or the platform provider will need to setup the facility in preparation for your groups. While every platform varies in process, at the very least they should have a mechanism or process for the following:

- Participant upload
- Push communications
- Discussion guide upload
- Visual stimuli upload or creation
- Administrative tools
- Interfaces for the moderator, participants, and observers
- Transcripts

Preparing Stimuli

Any visuals or research stimuli displayed in the discussion room are best setup beforehand so you can test how it appears in the platform. Anything you want to display in the facility that is not a typed question should be prepared in advance. Stimuli in a real-time chat can be used in a variety of ways, not just for what you may be testing. A limited list of possibilities includes:

- Your photo, company logo, or welcome video
- Facility instructions
- Who to contact for help
- Topics of discussion/change of topic
- Poll questions
- Sorting exercises
- Markup exercises
- Projective techniques

Check with your platform provider to determine the format required and the means of creating stimuli for the facility. Most facilities will have an "ideal" size for your graphics to display appropriately.

Real-time online can be an excellent environment for brainstorming, ideation, and other creative exercises. Stimuli presented to the group can be used as part of the creation exercise or to prompt creative thinking. Online, almost any type of stimuli is possible, from simple poll questions to markup exercises, from static images to live websites. Participants in real-time studies are already online, the entire web can be your playground!

Leveraging Unique Opportunities of Real Time

Beyond the advantages online qual research affords, real-time chat offers some unique perks to researchers:

- Candid, fleeting chatter = brutally honest comments
- Simultaneous response virtually eliminates the herd mentality
- Multiple simultaneous responses results in a large amount of data
- Real-time text encourages group interaction
- Clients are interested and engaged
- Lower costs overall

The very nature of real-time chat is that it is fleeting. Within seconds, if not minutes, comments scroll off the screen, welcoming new comments and perspectives with every movement. Participants in real-time chat are candid and forthcoming, often truthful to the point where the client may feel pain. As stressful as honest feedback may be for your client to receive, it's pure heaven for a qualitative researcher. Online chat will give you the opportunity to see and receive the good, the bad, and the ugly, shining a bright light on all those honest expressions.

Answering simultaneously also eliminates what is commonly referred to in traditional focus groups as the "herd mentality," where participants may alter their responses based on what they hear others say first. While not every answer appears on your screen at once, respondents all react to your question essentially at the same time.

Real-time chat is designed to receive *multiple* responses simultaneously, which produces an enormous amount of data in a short period of time. A transcript from a 90-minute group chat can easily be more than 15,000 words.

Once a participant in a real-time chat responds to the moderator's questions, she still has much to consider. Her screen quickly fills up with answers from other participants, to which she can then react and comment. From the participant's point of view, the chat is a constant stream of conversation in which she plays an active and vital role. When relaying expectations in your introduction to the group, state up-front if you want participants to interact and comment on other participants' responses.

Clients also catch the wave of energy of online chats, finding them not only convenient to view from home, but also exciting to be in-the-moment it's all happening. Unlike in-person focus groups, where the client in the back room has to wait patiently through every spoken word, online chat gives the client a free-flowing stream of answers to the most critical questions. Clients in real-time groups have a private area in which they can communicate with each other and collaborate with the moderator or group administrator, while watching the conversation from their own home or office.

The amount of labor required to complete an online chat is equivalent to an in-person group, as all the elements (screener, guide, moderating, report) are the same. However, total costs are reduced when travel and transcription expenses are completely eliminated.

Let's Get this Party Started

With a few deep breaths and a trip to the bathroom, you should be ready to moderate the online focus group. Your facility has been tested, your participants are coming in the door and your administrator is giving you the virtual thumbs-up. As you crack your fingers and begin to send your introduction to the group, it's *showtime*!

Your guide has been designed to fit the allotted time and establish an energy early on. As soon as you get to your warm-up questions, be ready to hit the gas with your probes. This is a critical moment when participants don't yet know what to expect and it's up to you to let them know. You want detail and you're going to ask until you get it.

TRAVEL TIP   **Overcrowding**

In the event of a large turnout, you may need to excuse some participants from the discussion. Be clear what your incentive payment policy is with the Administrator before he privately asks the participant to leave the room. You may want to ask the client ahead of time to prioritize the participant list and indicate who could be let go, if needed. If the client is online and observing, we recommend conferring with her before letting anyone go, although be prepared to make an executive decision if the client is not responding and you're having trouble managing so many participants at one time.

Probing one and all

While probing at the start is important to let participants know you're paying attention, it doesn't stop there. For every question you may have some participants who hold back and offer little to explain themselves. It's natural, so don't give up. They just need to understand what you want to know. Ask the question a different way, ask them privately or even ask them by phone after the group is over if you need to. If the platform you're using doesn't easily indicate who has responded, ask the group administrator to monitor and encourage those who did not respond to a previous question to do so. "No answer" is unacceptable, unless of course it comes with a full explanation!

Praise and move on

While it's important to let participants know you are human and paying attention, it's also important to let them know they are human and worth being paid attention to. Everyone needs a little praise and since you've done such a great job setting expectations, your participants are gushing with candid feedback. Let them know how much you appreciate it! *"You guys are doing a great job and the detail in your answers is very helpful, thank you!"* No need to overdo it, a little praise goes a long way. But definitely make note of the group's stellar performance and enlightening input. It will only inspire them to give you more.

Knowing when to let go

We know you're concerned about timing and you should be watching the clock as you move through the guide, but be ready and willing to dance a little and let the chat play out a bit. If it smells promising, and your client isn't putting up a virtual road block, go with your instincts and see what a new dance step does to the group. Sure, it may lead to nothing, but you tried. Now get back on track! You may need to make up for lost time by either combining or eliminating some future questions. We keep a paper version of the guide by the keyboard for quick reference and jotting notes. The guide displayed on a second monitor can serve a similar purpose.

Letting go also means shutting up. If participant responses include questions about the product or service you're testing, refrain from answering. You're not there to set them straight or to sell them anything; you're there to listen. Client observers may push you to answer, but hold tight and dig for more questions respondents may have. Questions participants pose can be the most insightful nuggets of all.

TRAVEL TIPS
Benefits of having help

Having someone function as the group administrator during your online focus group discussions can be immensely helpful. Online moderators typically have an assistant of some kind "in the room," who can be a member of the research team or the facility provider. Having someone monitor the frequency of participant responses and field client comments in real time affords the moderator complete and uninterrupted focus.

As the moderator, you want to be able to focus on probing participant responses. Distractions, like whether or not "Bob" has responded to your last question, can be alleviated if you have someone in the room to help you. The group administrator can also field and clarify client requests via private message so you can stay focused. Whoever you select as your group administrator, be clear on the role you'd like him to play in the room while you are moderating. Some other roles a live chat administrator can fill are:

- Welcome participants and answer preliminary questions.
- Monitor participants as they enter the room and contact by phone those who are missing.
- Welcome client observers in the back room and follow-up on any last-minute changes.
- Coordinate and test the visual stimuli to be displayed during the group.

- Coordinate and test the pre-loaded discussion guide questions.
- Alert the moderator at pre-determined times to stay on-track.
- Probe respondents for more detail during the live chat (dual-moderator role).
- Ensure participants are responding to each of the moderator's questions or probes.
- Attend to any user issues and technical difficulties during the live chat.
- Dismiss participants by request.
- Manage and remove disruptive participants, if needed.
- Field and clarify requests from client observers.
- Flag key comments during the live discussion.
- Note changes to the discussion guide that apply to future groups.
- Thank participants after the discussion has ended.
- Download the transcripts after the discussion has ended.
- Distribute incentives after the discussion has ended.

· · · · · ·

Practice makes perfect

Before going live, we recommend testing the facility and the features you intend to use. If the ability to practice is not inherent in the platform, ask your provider to set up a practice room where you can test your visual stimuli and ensure your guide questions are appearing correctly. Your client may want to have a test run before going live as well, so be sure everything is working with your provider first.

· · · · · ·

Last minute checklist

No matter how prepared you are, there's always something to forget. With all the focus on getting your client observers ready to go, it's easy to overlook some essential information you may need to quickly reference during the live group:

- Discussion guide (even though it's pre-loaded, have an extra copy somewhere)
- Participant screener and contact information
- Team contact information
- Facility links and logins
- Clock

· · · · · ·

Staying on-time

Real-time chat moderators run the risk of rushing questions due to the repetition and ultra-familiarity with the guide. It's important to keep a good pace throughout the discussion so participants can keep up, but are not bored waiting for you to ask the next question. Like a highway speed limit, keep up the pace, but don't have a lead foot.

Everyone has his or her own methods of staying on-track and on-time. Here are a few options to consider:

- When posting a question, take a moment and read it out loud as if you're reading it for the first time. This is how your participants are experiencing the question and it will keep you in-sync with the rhythm of their responses.

- Write the intended start time next to each section on your guide. When you get to each topic, check the clock and make adjustments to the rest of the guide accordingly. If you're just a few minutes behind, you may be able to make that up by combining or omitting future questions, or just by luck. If you're 10 minutes behind or more, you should private message your client observer. This is where knowing ahead of time which sections of your guide are most critical to cover will come in handy.

- Place an egg timer on your desk and set the minute limit for each section.

- Ask your group administrator to notify you if you go over in a particular section, or at certain intervals during the discussion.

If you're not sure, or your client isn't available, you're going to need to use your best judgment and make decisions quickly.

. . . . . .

Effective blinding

The concept of having participants answer your question before seeing the other respondents' answers is referred to as "blind answer mode." While well meaning in concept, when conducted in a real-time text chat environment, it can literally stop a discussion in its tracks. There are definitely times to use, and not to use, blind answer mode.

In an online focus group the scrolling chat has physical movement – the text appears, and moves up (or in some platforms down), and eventually off, the screen. In blind mode, the participant sees only their own response to the moderator's question. Beware! From the participant's perspective, this is like taking a moving car and downshifting from fifth to first. Like whiplash in an accident, participants begin to cry out:

"What happened?"

"Where did everyone go"

"Can you see this???"

The entire experience can take a great discussion into a tailspin, so use the "blind" mode carefully. In certain situations it can be quite helpful. For example, as participants are coming into the facility, having "blind answer mode" turned on enables you to talk privately with everyone simultaneously before the group. Similarly, putting everyone in blind answer mode before the group dismantles allows you to capture summary statements, final thoughts, or private musings from participants before they exit.

· · · · · ·

OMG & WTF situations

You name it; we've probably seen it. From clients flirting inappropriately in the back room (unaware that private conversations were logged in the transcript) to young boys overtly hitting on the female moderator. If you're uncomfortable, we probably have advice that will help.

&%$#@)$# great! – Some platforms today are outfitted with an anti-swear feature that will automatically bleep out swear words in comments as they are posted. Whether the platform knows bad language or not, your platform will most likely have the option of muting or even excusing a participant for inappropriate behavior during a live discussion.

I love what you're wearing – Online chat has a tendency to get people talking and really let their hair down. Sometimes in those situations, as the moderator, you may find yourself dampening little flirt fires, You may have to message participants privately, to stay on topic. If behavior becomes too friendly between participants, you can ask them privately to cease or exit, or push them out politely, if needed.

Just between you and me – Another hazard of online chat can be the unexpected reveal of something personal. Caught up in the discussion, participants may share personal information that they had not intended to blurt out. Like a loud toot in church, these comments are best left unattended and a change of subject may help reduce the swelling shock.

. . . . . .

Private Message overload

In an online focus group the client has private access to the moderator. This is both an advantage and a potential aneurysm, so plan effectively. In our experience this is where the group administrator plays a vital role as the messenger between you and the client observers.

If a client observer sends a private request to "skip this," it may not be clear which "this" she is referring to. In those situations, the group administrator would receive the message, know it was not clear, and reply back for more information. Only when the direction is solid will the admin relay the message to the moderator, who up until this point has been blissfully unaware and focused on the group chat, undeterred by the private conversations going on behind the scenes.

If you invite multiple members of the client team to observe the online focus group it is even more important to establish rules of communication with the moderator during the live chat. First, identify who on the team will speak for the group. Without this assignment, observers could message conflicting directions. Let them confer in their private channel first, if needed, and provide an agreed-upon direction the administrator can review and pass along.

Debrief with the client

Reconvening with your client after each group, either by chat or phone, will help clarify and confirm any guide adjustments that should be considered for future groups. Changes to the guide or visual stimuli can often be made between groups, if needed.

A Week in the Life of a Real-Time Chat Project

Thursday, after recruiting complete and group scheduled

- Call group administrator and confirm availability for Wednesday evening.
- Check-in with platform provider for login access and to confirm setup procedure.
- The recruiter sends final spreadsheet.
- Send recommended selections to the client (client replies with a request to replace some of the selects so there's a better mix of incomes).
- Remind client you need the video files for testing before Wednesday.
- Begin draft of discussion guide based on research objectives and priorities noted in prior client discussions.

Friday

- Email the client a second pass at the final selects (this time she approves).
- Remind client you need the video files for testing before Wednesday.
- Access the platform and upload selected recruits (opt to assign each a generic username to maintain participant anonymity).
- Confirm with platform provider no identifiable information (PII) will be visible to others in the chat room (this has happened to you before).
- Email attendees access instructions from the platform.
- Send first draft discussion guide to client.
- Breathe, the process is underway!

Saturday and Sunday

- Shouldn't you be working on that other proposal due Monday?

Monday

- Check email, as well as any messages within the platform to locate undeliverable emails or questions sent from invited participants.
- Remind client you need the video files for testing before Wednesday.
- Remind client to provide you the list of observers to invite and schedule a call to discuss the guide with the team tomorrow.

Tuesday

- Great call with the client! Priorities more clear, so move around a couple sections in the guide as a result and re-send for final approval.
- Receive list of observers from client, upload into platform, and invite.
- Receive videos and upload them into the platform for display during the group.
- Connect with group administrator, confirm facility access, start time and special instructions (big group of client observers has been challenging to manage in the past).

Wednesday

- Receive final guide approval and upload into the platform.
- Call the group administrator and review the guide and client priorities.
- Test the chat facility and all moderator controls.
- Reminder calls to invited participants (reconfirm start time in their time zone).
- Print a copy of the guide for the desk (you find this easier to follow).
- Piddle.
- Login several minutes early and welcome participants as they enter.
- Begin the first session.
- Client de-brief between groups.
- Slight modification to the guide, so your administrator uploads the changes for next group.
- Begin the second session.
- Download and email transcripts to the client.
- Download and email list of active participants to the recruiter.

Thursday

- Review transcripts and prepare analysis.

Friday

- Distribute incentives to participants.
- Deliver topline report to client.
- Congratulate yourself for a job well done!

CHAPTER 10

Extended-Time Moderating Online

[Managing the multi-day trip]

As you have browsed around in this book so far, you have seen how much variation is truly possible in online qualitative. You can design almost anything, just as you can with in-person research. For this section, we are going to work from the most common extended design of a project that starts and wraps within one week. Once you have the basics under control, you can plan for longer engagements. The key to remember throughout is that human beings are going to be experiencing this. Focus on how the participants will experience the project, and you will have a successful study.

Project Timelines

The timelines for **recruiting** are the same as you would expect for an in-person qualitative project. The only differences are these:

- You will usually want all of the recruits identified a day or two in advance of the project launch date in order to get people loaded in to the platform (see below) and get log-in information out to them.
- It is sometimes helpful to let people log-in early, before the study starts, to say hello, confirm that they have no technical issues, upload their photo or pick an avatar.
- Occasionally, you might be confirming their ability to use the mobile or video functions in advance, and asking for an early log-in for that reason.

Just be sure you have given clear dates and deadlines to your recruiter. Sometimes you need to replace a recruit after the project has started. You will want to be clear how far into a multi-day project you are prepared to accept newcomers.

People who show up after the first day can be inclined to rush through the questions to "catch up." They have not been part of the introductory sections, so they aren't as connected to the rest of the group as the others. These folks are likely to interact less with the other participants, and treat the whole discussion as an individual activity. As always with qualitative, a great deal of your success is dependent on the quality of your recruiting, and whether or not people show up.

Typical timelines for three days of content

Some typical timelines for a project of one-week duration are shown in the table below. Both of these projects have the same participant time commitment, generally 1.5 to 2 hours.

Typical One Week Timetables for Two Projects

	Project A Tuesday through Thursday Project	Project B Monday through Friday Project
Fri	Send out log-in IDs.	Send out log-in IDs.
Sat		
Sun		
Mon	Send out reminder about next day start.	Send out reminder that study is open. Launch first set of topics allowing two days to complete.
Tue	Launch first set of topics	
Wed	Launch second set of topics.	Launch second set of topics.
Thu	Launch final topics.	Launch final topics, allowing two days to complete.
Fri	Wrap up any stragglers.	
Sat	Close forum.	Permit stragglers to wrap up through the weekend.
Sun		Close forum.

In Project A, the discussion is focused on Tuesday, Wednesday, and Thursday.

In Project B, the discussion starts on Monday, but there is more flexibility for participants to complete the first set of topics. Likewise, the final set of topics allows two days for completion. If you are going to ask for a specific activity to occur during the project – for example, go shopping, try a frozen food product, visit a bank branch – you need to allow time during the schedule for this.

From the perspective of managing your own time, Project A gives you a more focused active moderation window, and may be easier for clients to follow along. Project B provides more flexibility for you and for the respondents, but means you will need to monitor activity across a bigger participation time window.

Stragglers

You see that we have allowed for "stragglers." Participants often have events in their lives that interfere with participation, even when they are motivated and engaged. Cars break down, kids get sick, computers stop working, and life happens! You should assume that you will get some requests to finish the project "late," and decide how you will handle them. In particular, B2B participants often will have their plans change after they commit to participating, and it's nice to let them complete all the activities rather than lose a contribution.

Having people finish the project late is not usually as problematic as having them start the project late, because it has less impact on the group dynamics. One cautionary note: you are likely to have sequenced the questions quite deliberately, and this participant is now out of that sequence. For example, maybe you wanted to conclude a discussion about current brand impressions before showing new concepts. You will want to ensure your straggler doesn't engage with the topics out of order. Depending on your platform, there are various ways to manage this. The simplest of all, of course, is just to ask your participant to do it this way: "Hi Freda, it's no problem finishing the topics on Saturday. When you come back, please be sure to do Section 2 before you do Section 3 – it's important to see these topics in the right order. Thanks, and see you later!"

Basic Logistics

There are a few things you need to figure out fairly early. They are not complicated, but it's like traveling – if you forget to pack shoes, you will be kicking yourself (with your bare feet) when you get to the hotel.

You will have access to the project space in advance of the "go-live" date and time. Different providers vary in their policies, so be sure you know how much time you have to get things set up.

Before anyone arrives, you have three key tasks to manage:

1. Create and load the discussion guide including all the questions and all stimuli.
2. Load in the participants and any observers.
3. Create invitation communications to send out log-in information and get everyone on board.

Your platform provider can support all of these activities to some degree, but let's assume you are in full DIY mode for the purposes of this chapter. The more you know about how the system works, the better you can plan.

Inputting the guide

Once you have chosen a platform and had the full tour, you will know how to load in a discussion guide. This is going to happen one question at a time, entering data into an online form. Common options include giving the question a name (e.g., "Welcome"), actual question text, and timing. Timing is simply the date and time the question goes live, i.e. becomes visible to participants. Questions are typically grouped into clusters of topics, with one or more topic going live on a specific day on the project.

Once the discussion forum is open to participants, they can log in at any time of day or night, so you need to specify exactly when topics are available to be answered. In practice, this is not as complicated as it sounds. It's no more complicated than searching for airline tickets online.

You will also be specifying question types, and options such as one-on-one, blind, or open, for each question. Some platforms will let you specify whether or not the participants can edit their response after posting. The actual words or stimuli in a question can usually be edited at any time. Other question options can only be edited before someone answers the question. So there is lots of flexibility to make changes.

PRO TIP

It is common to have multiple groups running simultaneously. Most platforms will let you create one guide, then copy it to another group. Try to make most of your edits before you make the copy, to minimize your work. You may need to tweak the language of your questions a bit for different segments.

Don't forget the stimuli

You may choose to add the stimuli after putting the basic guide in, for a few reasons. You may not actually *have* the stimuli from your client yet, despite giving them a firm deadline (just like in face-to-face!). You may have to create some of the stimuli yourself, with projective exercises. You may want to add some video of yourself to the question, and want to wait until you have combed your hair and are out of your PJs to create the video. Fortunately, the platform is a computer with infinite patience, and it will let you edit and tweak to your heart's content, at all hours of the day or night.

Loading participant information

Your recruiter will have provided you a spreadsheet, just as for any other project. You'll work with this, creating a basic participant profile for everyone in the project. The basics are name and email address, but you may also have the option of including segment or other profile information, e.g., demographics like age and gender, location, product usage.

Platforms vary quite a lot in how they handle this aspect, so it is good to ask enough questions to be sure you understand how the system works. A few questions you will want to be clear on are shown here.

1. What information is visible to observers, and what is visible to other participants?
2. Which fields can be changed after creating the participant? If you make a typo in the spelling of a name, do you need to create a new participant, or can you just edit that after?
3. Can you assign a fake name or ID if you need to in order to preserve anonymity of the participants?
4. How are participant passwords assigned? Can they change them after they log in?

Observers

Observers have a log-in ID, but no profiling information. They will be able to see everything you post, and everything the participants post. They can make "back room" posts that are visible to you as the moderator, but not visible to the participants. These are often called comments, and can be useful to high-light interesting topics, or raise a potential follow-up question.

TRAVEL TIP   Protecting anonymity

Just because you are online does not mean you are anonymous, even if only first names are visible. Consider small populations of professionals, for example. You may think this is unlikely, but then you'll be really surprised when it happens, as it has to us.

It may not matter that participants recognize each other, but you also need to offer them protection from being recognized by the observers, particularly in B2B studies, or studies involving highly visible individuals, e.g., wealthy donors to charity.

The solution is straightforward – simply use a reduced version of the name, or some other artificial ID. While we prefer using randomly assigned anonymous first names, moderators have reported using movie star names, literary figures, fictional heroes, or the names of colors, tree species, or gemstones. If you choose to use artificial names, you will quickly see we humans add meaning to abso-lutely everything. Oaks and willows and cactus trees are not just trees, they are symbolic of attributes. Try to avoid making your participants wear a name that feels like ill-fitting clothing they wouldn't choose for themselves. If you have the time and patience, let them choose their own screen name, and their own avatar.

The human tendency to share information can inadvertently reveal identi-ties, despite your best efforts. This comes out most frequently in introductory questions, where the carefully disguised individual then puts in a post revealing details like, "Hi, I'm Bill, I'm a retired IT entrepreneur and I launched a global foun-dation with my wife Melinda, and we're really interested in polio eradication also play some pretty competitive bridge with my buddy Warren." Oops.

No worries. As the moderator of an extended discussion, you have god-like powers, and can carefully edit these little slips. If you do make an edit, just be sure to send a note to the participant explaining why.

If for some reason the kimono does fall open, and someone feels a little too re-vealed in an uncomfortable way, of course you want to handle this with care and respect, just as you would in face-to-face. These are times when having access to ethical guidelines and a community of colleagues are really invaluable.

Inviting everyone on board

When you send out the log-in information, a good practice is to reinforce the timing and participation expectations, as well as set the tone for the study. Recruiters sometimes suggest that they should send out the log-in information, and you can certainly have them do this if you prefer. If the recruiter is associated with the platform provider, this may be a nice time-saver for you. For the most part, we prefer it when log-in information can be sent to recruits directly from the platform, and here's why:

1. Each log-in ID and password is unique to each participant.

The platform is set up to make issuing log-in information straightforward. It's generally much easier to handle these communications from inside the platform. If the independent recruiter issues the log-ins, you will need to give them the entire list. Their concern is that people get the information in a timely manner, and that they have a good show rate. So let them know when people should expect the information, and who you haven't heard from yet. Agree on what follow-up is appropriate.

2. You want to be sure your emails are reaching the participant.

A simple way to do this is to ask them to confirm receipt with a quick email response or even a phone call. This starts a nice pattern of having them interact with you as the moderator and you can easily deal with any questions that arise. If there are any technical issues, you can get the platform provider to troubleshoot these, e.g., they have an out-of-date web browser. Sometimes a participant wants to use a different email for study communications, and they usually choose to tell you at this point. Fortunately, you have time to make changes!

In B2B studies, we have found that corporate firewalls can sometimes filter out communications coming from the platform. If you know this early on, you can manage it in a couple of different ways. Start by talking to your platform provider to help you problem solve. In the worst case, you can send the information directly from one of your own emails, or you can send it to their personal email address. Having an alternate participant email address in your recruiting grid can be helpful. A phone number is also a helpful useful backup.

3. You want to reinforce that all study communication is coming from you.

If you think about a face-to-face facility, once people are escorted into the room, you are the one managing the show. The same thing is true online. The directions about how to be a good participant should be coming from you.

When online research was a new thing, moderators sometimes chose to place a quick call to all the participants to say hello. The purpose of such a call is to share your warmest, friendliest moderator voice, to let people know that there is a real person on the other end of your typing, and to deal with any questions or vague worries that may be present. Making such calls does take time, and is probably not needed by most people in developed markets, for them to feel comfortable. However, It is a nice touch and if you are in any doubt about how people may be feeling at the start of a project, a quick phone call can put them at ease. For B2B projects, this is an opportunity to reinforce just what kind of information you will be asking people to share and how it will be handled, especially if sensitive topics are being discussed, for example, how the organization manages hiring, or manages technology buying, or manages innovation.

TRAVEL TIP
Should you reveal your regular email address?

Opinions vary on this topic. Here are just a few of the things we have encountered after an extended study has concluded and the participants had our regular email address. Participants write asking why they have not yet received their incentive – a communication you probably want going through the recruiter. Participants write you at a later date to tell you about a problem they are having with the sponsor of the study and ask for your help to resolve it. Participants add you to their email distribution list for a newsletter. Participants have even invited us to be friends or link-up on a social network.

The only reason to reveal your actual full identity, in our experience, is to create credibility with a high-status target group, e.g., very senior executives. These are the same people that you might give a business card in a face-to-face interview.

Without participants, we can't make a living, so we have the utmost respect for them in all their varieties and quirky humanity. But that does not mean we want an ongoing relationship. If you are not going to communicate exclusively through the platform's communications tools, consider creating a new email address used only for study purposes.

Crafting Your Discussion Guide

Just as with a face-to-face research activity, you are going to plan and manage the difficulty of the topics and the energy of the group. During the early topics, you want things to be easy and friendly, and to set the tone for the rest of the interactions. Any questions that you want a top-of-mind reaction to should go early, before a lot of thinking on the subject has occurred.

On a standard project, the second day of content is usually the heaviest and most demanding of participants. This might be going deeper into a topic, asking for more detailed information, or perhaps reactions to concepts. The third day of content should be a little lighter, perhaps offer a twist on what's already been said, and pull in any new questions that have arisen.

First day

- Welcome
- Introduction to topic and individual experiences

Second day

- The meatiest part of your guide goes here
- Reactions to new concepts

Third day

- Refocus on interesting areas
- Wrap up loose ends
- Thank everyone and close

While you want to plan your whole guide in advance, we would encourage you to expect to make changes in the second and third day's questions based on early learning, just as you would in a real-time encounter. If you ask wonderful questions that trigger rich responses, you may not need some planned questions.

Leave participants time on the third day to refocus on some area that is not yet clear, or where new issues were raised. This is often more productive than trying to get people to "go back" and answer follow-up questions.

It is very easy to expand your topics beyond what you promised at the time of recruiting. Engaged clients will also want more topics introduced as they start learning. And although your platform will expand to accommodate any number of new topics, your participants will not. By the end, they may think the tour has been great, but their feet are getting tired and they don't want to look at any more museums, no matter how great the art is.

In face-to-face projects, and in real-time projects, the clock is always in front of you, keeping you from going overboard on any given topic. In extended projects, you must be this clock, protecting the time and energy of your participants for the most important – and only the most important – additions to the guide.

Leverage the unique opportunities

With clever design, you can get the best of all worlds – the depth of an in-depth interview, controlled responses to stimuli uncontaminated by group effects, and also group interaction.

Go deep with everyone

The extended online environment permits *everyone* to answer every question in any amount of detail. This is one of the most exciting and productive aspects of this form of research, so you will want to capitalize on it. In a face-to-face setting, everyone cannot tell their full story of how they researched and bought their car, got diagnosed and treated for a serious illness, or made an important career change. In this kind of face-to-face situation, a five-minute story from each of 8 people will take at least 40 minutes! But you can take the time for this online in extended discussions. Asking for these kinds of detailed stories can provide incredibly rich information and let you tease out very useful insights.

Combine individual interviews with group interactions

You can make some sections private and invite participants to share private personal details only with you. This is typically called one-to-one or diary mode.

This can let participants share moments that might be uncomfortable in a face-to-face setting. Even in the online environment, some topics will not be shared with a group, for fear of experiencing negative judgments from others. For example, in an online diary, a dog owner shared the problem that her dog pooped on the deck. She has tried any number of interventions, and was very frustrated by this problem. This was only raised in the diary portion, which was one-on-one with the moderator, and did not come up at all in the group discussions, even when talking about related topics.

Your participants are in their own environment

Participants are prompted and reminded of things by their immediate environment, whether they are engaging from home, office, or out of the home. They have access to actual reference material beyond their memories. So you can ask them to take a picture of their medicine cabinet, for example. Or just to look in their freezer and tell you what brands of frozen pizza are in there right now. In face-to-face, these kinds of exercises rely heavily on memory, and will definitely be influenced by the group's responses.

Use the tools to manage group effects

For any kind of concept or creative testing, questions in "blinded" mode will give you an initial response to the stimulus on an individual level, and then let you see the impact of the group discussion on concept reactions. Or you can have people look at, and react to, all the stimuli before entering into a group discussion. These are controls that you really do not have in face-to-face groups.

Managing energy, effort and focus

In a multi-day discussion, one of your biggest considerations is how to manage the energy of the individual participants. This is true for face-to-face research, as well, of course. Here are a few of the things to consider:

Start easy

Start with easy topics that everyone can easily answer, planning to use this time to learn more about the people in the project and also establish norms for responding in appropriate detail.

Balance difficult with easy, boring with fun

Some topics are heavier lifting than others. When people have been working hard for you, plan to give them a break by doing something fun. Avoid stacking too many tough questions together, unless there is a natural flow to the topic.

For example, if you ask people to tell you about all of their vitamins and supplements, listing each one, what they use it for, what brand they buy, and how they got started using it, that is a demanding question. You should have a clear idea of how much time will be involved in answering. A question like the vitamin one I just posed will take at least 20 minutes to answer, perhaps more.

So your next question might be a little lighter and easier. For example, in the vitamin study, you might ask which retailer is likely to have the latest and greatest supplements. Or which has the best selection of their preferred brands. This is the type of question that is more likely to generate interaction, as well. This type of interaction is like a reward – it is a little nugget of learning for participants, and like us, their brains thrive on new information.

Projective exercises tend to be fun, although they can also require fairly focused thinking. Activities involving pictures are always more fun. You can use pictures even when there is no particular need for a stimulus. For example, you could post an image of clouds scudding across a blue sky to signal a topic requiring imagination.

Signal shifts in activities

The exception to the balancing rule is sandwiching the wrong things together. Trust us, this is an easy mistake to make. You have people rolling along doing a lot of left-brain type activities about supplement-buying behavior and organic manufacturing concerns. To give them a break, you throw in a picture projective, such as, "Pick three pictures that describe the way your supplements make your body feel and tell me about them." This juxtaposition may actually result in a screeching, putting-on-the-brakes noise that you will be able to hear across the room!

When you are going to shift the activities, it's a good idea to signal this with a communication that does not require a response. Just as you would in face-to-face, say something like, *"Thanks for all the great work on the last few questions, I know some of this is kind of hard work. So we are going to shift to a different kind of topic, I think you will find this interesting! Please go to the next topic!"*

Design as if you were moderating

When you are designing your questions and flow, you need to put yourself in the moment that has not yet happened, and really pretend that you are moderating in real time. Hear the words in your head. Imagine answering the questions.

In a real-time project, while you need to plan, you can also adjust on the fly. In extended, you must make your topics and activities so clear and obvious that no adjustments are needed. Of course, in practice, this never happens. But try to anticipate every little area of confusion or uncertainty and resolve it in advance.

One experienced online moderator we know has told us she thinks of the design stage of asynchronous projects as moderating. This is a great mindset to adopt.

Manage time requirements carefully

When you recruited people to the project, you gave them an indication of how much time the study would require. You might have said something like, "log in twice a day, first to respond to the topics yourself, and then later to respond to what others have posted and any follow-up questions I asked."

One of the challenges of getting people engaged with the group is that they will want to read what others have said. Plus you may ask them to do this, to read and respond. Reading takes time. And the longer and more detailed the responses, the more time it takes. This can be one reason to do really lengthy topics in one-to-one mode. If you anticipate a lot of detailed responses, then you may want to keep your group sizes a little smaller to reduce the reading burden.

If you think reading is becoming a problem for people, you can suggest that they just follow a few people in the discussion, and not try to read everything.

Any question that involves an assignment of some kind, such as a shopping assignment, a cooking task, trying out a different personal care product, takes time. You must respect the time commitment you have promised people.

Frequently, this means managing your client's expectations about how many new questions or topics can be added. Consider concept testing. In a focus group, we might try to limit discussion to six or eight concepts. Clients may assume that an extended-time online study can accommodate fifteen concepts or more, which is a lot of reading and reacting and can really wring the energy out of the group. If you must do something like that, be sure to give people breaks.

Decisions of any kind take psychic energy – no, we don't mean the supernatural kind, we mean simple brainpower. Just look at the mental energy you expend managing your email every day!

Balance interaction with blind and one-on-one questions

A one-on-one question in an extended discussion is like pulling the participant out of the group environment into a private interview room. A blind question is more akin to asking participants to do an individual exercise, then share their answers with the group.

If you post all questions in "blind" mode, your participants will experience an environment where they are always the first one to answer. That is not what you as the moderator will see, but that is how it will feel to them. It's just not as engaging as landing on an activity and getting a chance to see what others have said, then adding your own thoughts.

One-on-one questions are similarly isolating. This can be a good thing, but also means that you as the moderator must provide energy that the group might otherwise provide.

Keep it short

Different moderators have different styles, but we have a definite view on this topic. People do not read long questions. People hate long questions. Long questions represent a failure to simplify and cut out the unnecessary words.

Ask fewer, bigger questions

In a threaded discussion, your environment is going to look something like the following – platforms vary, of course; some have a more vertical approach to navigation than shown here. You might have a couple of topics each day, and each topic will have multiple questions nested within it.

Topic One: My Vitamins and Supplements							
Question 1	Question 2	Question 3	Question 4	Question 5	Question 6	Question 7	Question 8

Welcome to the first day of our discussion. To get things started, please tell me . . .

1. What are all the different types of vitamins and supplements you use?

Let's think about our hypothetical vitamin and supplement study again. Perhaps you want to know a lot about usage and consumption patterns before you get into some specific topics related to brand image and maybe new marketing concepts. The table below shows two approaches to getting a baseline on this information.

Q	Approach A: Lots of "little" questions	Approach B: A few "big" questions
1	What are all the different types of vitamins and supplements you use?	To get started, please tell me the story of the vitamins and supplements in your life. • What are you and your family using, and how did this come to be? I'd really like to hear as much detail about this as you can share – what brands you buy now, what different supplements and vitamins you use, and anything else that feels relevant here.
2	Have you always used these types of supplements, or have you used others in the past?	If I were visiting your home for a week, and quietly observing how you and your family use vitamins and supplements, **what would I see every day, and on different days of the week?**
3	And what brands of vitamins and supplements do you prefer?	Imagine I'm still visiting your home, car, and even where you work and secretly snooping around. Where all would I find YOUR vitamins and supplements? What about the REST OF YOUR FAMILY? (As always, please tell me as much as you can about this. I would love it if you have time to post some photos) *Hint: you don't have to repeat yourself if you already answered part of this.*
4	Have you always used these brands, or have you changed brands, and what prompted the change?	

Q	Approach A: Lots of "little" questions	Approach B: A few "big" questions
5	Do you choose the vitamins and supplements for others in your family, and are these different than what you choose for yourself?	
6	When do you take your vitamins and supplements, and at what times of day? Is this different on different days of the week, or times of the year?	
7	And what about your family . . . when do they take their vitamins and supplements, and at what times of the day? And is this different on different days of the week or times of the year?	
8	Are you tired of these questions yet?	

What you will find in the approach shown as A is that your participants, trying to be helpful, will answer some of the later questions while answering an early question. They are very likely to start answering question A2 when they answer question A1. They might say something like this:

"I recently started buying Green Label, which is the store brand, and I really like it for me. I have always used Flintstones for the kids, and I used to use them too, when the kids were little. But now I want something a little more potent."

However, when your participant gets to the question A2, they may say something along these lines:

"As I mentioned in the earlier question, I used to get Flintstones for the kids, and I took them myself because it was just easier than buying a lot of different things. But now I want something different, and I am taking the Green Label organics, like I mentioned. I like the Organic, and it has more of some of the specific nutrients I'm looking for, like zinc."

You can see the problem here, right? The questions, and the responses, are going to start becoming repetitive for both of you. You are spending precious study time getting duplicate information.

While by no means perfect, we have found that approach B usually works better in extended-time studies online. When you write the topic, you will anticipate opportunities to ask probing follow-up questions to flesh out specific areas of interest.

If you are saying to yourself *"Those questions are a lot longer!"* that is true. Traveling through the city of insights as a moderator is always really like riding a unicycle – keeping your balance, and avoiding potholes is a big part of the journey and a big part of the joy.

Use platform way-finders effectively

Your online platform will have all kinds of ways for you to point people in the right direction. Consider giving your topics evocative names. Consider using names for questions, instead of numbers. For example, Question B1 above could be "The Story", and B2 could be "My home" or "Week in the life." If people can see what topics are coming along, they can be intrigued, and also have a better idea of where you are going.

Topic One: My Vitamins and Supplements							
The Story	Week in the Life	Snooping	Question 4	Question 5	Question 6	Question 7	Question 8

Welcome to the first day of our discussion. To get things started, please tell me ...

What are all the different types of vitamins and supplements you use?

Within each question, you are likely to have formatting options including color, highlighting, size of type, bullet points, icons, bold, italics, and brackets to help people understand your focus. Compare the two examples here to see how this can work.

Q	No formatting	Lots of formatting
BS	Imagine I'm still visiting your home, car, and even where you work and secretly snooping around. Where are all the places I would find your vitamins and supplements? What about the rest of your family? As always, please tell me as much as you can about this. I would love it if you have time to post some photos. Hint: you don't have to repeat yourself if you already answered part of this.	Imagine I'm still visiting your home, car, and even where you work and secretly snooping around. • **Where are all the places I would find YOUR vitamins and supplements?** • **What about the REST OF YOUR FAMILY?** As always , please tell me as much as you can about this. I would love it if you have time to post some photos. *[Hint: you don't have to repeat yourself if you already answered part of this.]*

Keep in mind that some people are scanners, and will only read the most important parts of the question. Make sure they can quickly **see** the most important parts by manipulating the font size and color, by using color, type size, and bold face. Icons and images always add a friendly element when you can do this.

Like the P.S. in a direct mail piece, using a hint judiciously at the end of a question can provide helpful tips without loading down the question with text.

If you use some of the formatting options consistently, it will make life easier for your participants, who will know quickly what you are looking for them to do.

The virtual smile

As you plan and format your guide, you will start to craft your own personal style. This is a good thing. Every moderator develops a unique style and approach that works for them, and online is the same.

We like to show people our virtual smiles and, we try to build as much empathy as possible. We use all the tools at our disposal to communicate unconditional positive regard, and to invite playful participation. That includes humor, selective self-disclosure, emoticons (which are the stickers of the virtual world, and we love stickers!), and anything else that helps people relax, engage, and tell us more. These are adjusted to fit the participant group of course – you will use a different style with a group of corporate executives than with a group of frozen entrée lovers – but it should still feel like your presence is showing through in the topic guide.

Actively Moderating the Extended Project

In extended online projects, quite a bit of the moderating actually happens during the design phase of the project, as you have seen. This section will look at what happens once you "go live."

The big moment has arrived, you've sweated over your guide, you've loaded your participants, everything is "go," the day has come, your project is "live." Woo hoo! You log in to your forum and start clicking around to see what is happening.

Well, there's a good chance that nothing is happening yet. Do not panic. With asynchronous, you will find that it takes a while for things to get going. This can be very anxiety producing, but is a normal state of affairs. Real time online projects are like real-time in-person projects in that there is a definite moment when things start. In extended projects, the start often feels a bit ragged. The tour bus is there, ready to roll, but no one has boarded yet. It may feel like nothing is happening, until, all of a sudden, you find that a ton of stuff is happening!

Here's what a week in the life of the moderator might look like in an extended-time online project. We'll use the same design we used earlier, for a three-day project happening mid-week.

Project A Tuesday through Thursday Project	
Fri	Send out log-in IDs.
Sat	
Sun	
Mon	Send out reminder about next day start.
Tue	Launch first set of topics.
Wed	Launch second set of topics.
Thu	Launch final topics.
Fri	Wrap up any stragglers.
Sat	Close forum.
Sun	

A Week in the Life of an Extended Project

Thursday, before the study starts

- Have a good look at the last grid from the recruiter – even though we still need one more name, you decide to load in the ones already confirmed.
- Receive final changes to the guide from client. Remind client you need graphics for the Wednesday topics.
- Write the introductory email that will go out Friday.
- Create a short section of the online guide that will "go live" on Friday. It is called "Before the study starts" and just has instructions about how to navigate, how to change a password, and how to upload a photo or select an avatar. Participants are encouraged to post a quick hello.

Friday, before the study starts

- Recruiter sends a note asking when the log-ins are going to go out, and you say "I'm on it," and get on it.
- Log-in IDs go out by noon, with a request to acknowledge via quick email reply. Some emails start coming in. Take a highlighter and note on your paper copy of the grid who has acknowledged.
- Check that the "Before the study starts" section is "live" to participants.
- Finish loading in the discussion guide. Decide to leave the last day mostly unstructured, because it might change.
- Check the forum. Notice that two participants have logged in and so you say "hello, thanks for logging in. See you next week!"

Saturday and Sunday

- Your reward for good planning is to get the weekend off!

Monday

- Send out an email reminder (from the platform) reminding people what the schedule looks like, and say you are looking forward to seeing them the next day.
- Add any final participants to the platform, and send out the introductory communications.
- Note any participants who have not logged in or sent you a confirming email. Either ask recruiter to check in with them or phone them yourself to confirm they got the log-in. Troubleshoot as needed.
- Check that first set of topics will go live as promised. Remind yourself that some participants are in a time zone east of yours, and set the start time earlier.
- Obsessively review the sequencing on the topics. Log in as a participant to ensure things look the way they are supposed to look.
- Decide to record a short welcome video. Write a brief script, smile for the camera, and upload it to the landing page. Play video several times, admiring your creativity – the project will be awesome!

Tuesday

- Get up, make a coffee, check the forum.
- Monitor almost continuously. As each person arrives, post a personal response to them.

- See that one of your questions is causing confusion. Go in and edit the question, noting in brackets (edited) so that early responders don't think they hallucinated it. Send previous responders a quick email through the platform asking them to have another look at the question.
- Post frequently, praising all responses, but highlighting in particular the behavior you want others to emulate.
- Grab a quick lunch, check email, but keep a close eye on your forum all day.
- Pull out a couple of juicy quotes and send them to the client.
- Finish posting the rest of the discussion guide.
- Obsessively check times and sequencing, paying particular attention to topics that have blind or one-on-one sections, or that only go to specific segments.
- Have dinner, and then check the forum again. You note that a lot of people are participating now that they are home from their work day.
- Post a new topic thanking people for their participation, and reminding them that new topics will be posted on Wednesday. Send out an email with a similar positive message.
- Spouse calls you to come to bed; it's late. You post a final note saying you have to sign off now, but you promise to read everything you missed in the morning.

Wednesday

- Get up, make a coffee, check the forum.
- Confirm that today's topics loaded as planned.
- Read and acknowledge to everything posted after you went to bed.
- Have a conference call with the client team. This was planned and scheduled a week ago, and team members were assigned individual monitoring tasks. Decide how to deal with follow-up questions that have come up. Client wants to change some of the stimuli for Thursday. You say okay, but remind them you need this material soon in order to post it.
- Monitor and respond to everyone. Probe little but be present lots.
- Troubleshoot any non-responders, keeping in mind that they may be planning to log in later in the day, after work and family obligations are done.
- Send a few individual emails to strong contributors thanking them for their participation.

- Make final changes to Thursday topics, load any new stimuli.
- Spouse asks if you are coming to bed. You say goodnight, promising to read everything in the morning.

Thursday

- Get up, make a coffee, check the forum.
- Confirm that today's topics loaded as planned.
- Decide to post another video thanking everyone for their participation and excellent contributions to the topics.
- Check in with client.
- Review your objectives and ensure you have the material you need to cover everything. Revisit any gaps with a short new topic you add. Send an email to anyone who may not have seen that late addition.
- Communicate directly with anyone having trouble finishing the project.
- Be present and visible often, but post relatively little.
- Thank everyone for their participation.

Friday

- Confirm incentive payments with recruiter.
- Close off access to those that have finished, leaving open only for people who promised to finish up.
- Once final responses are in, close access to the forum. Topics are no longer "live," but you and the observers can still read everything.
- Pat yourself on the back, the fieldwork is done.

You are probably swimming in data, but you did a great job. Everyone said they enjoyed the experience, and your client has already learned a lot. There's still the analysis of course, but the fieldwork is finished.

Probing, Praising & Rapport Building

As you can see from our week in the life example above, there are some specific activities we recommend for active moderation during fieldwork in extended projects. No matter how good your online discussion guide, the group does not moderate itself any more than an in-person focus group does. Many of the same tools are used to generate great contributions, but they are used a little differently.

Praise early and often

It is basically impossible to go overboard with praise. During the early parts of the discussion, it is a good practice to acknowledge everyone's first post of the day. *("Hi, Amir, good to see you here. Thanks for logging in and posting.")*

You also want to make particular acknowledgments of the most detailed responses on topic. *("Thanks so much for really giving me lots of detail on this topic, Naomi. These detailed answers are so helpful for me to understand the topic. EVERYONE: please don't worry about saying too much, I want to hear from everyone in as much detail as you can.")*

The first post on a new topic area is often another time to acknowledge someone stepping in first. *("Thanks for getting us started on this topic, Andrea. I'm sure others will weigh in soon. Anyone else?")*

A quick thank-you at the end of each major topic, or the end of each day, is always appreciated. Sometimes people will thank you right back, which is a good indicator that things are going well.

Building rapport — more virtual smiling

One way to build rapport is selective disclosure. This is something most good moderators do easily in person. You reveal yourself as a person, but not in a way that biases opinions. It's tricky, in one way, because you need to be cautious about what you say. During introductions, for example, you might acknowledge the cute puppy photo your participant posted, *"What a cutie! I'm a sucker for puppies. How old is Rover now?"* You probably would not say, *"I love dogs too. In fact, I compete in dog agility events with our purebred Australian Sheep Dogs."*

Find safe topics to just get people talking in the introduction phase. *("Welcome, Sandy. I see you are from Colorado – I heard you are getting a lot of snow there right now?")*

Use unconditional positive regard to respond to all viewpoints. If someone introduces themselves in a way that is really hard to identify with, you can still respond positively. *"It's always so great having a diversity of views, and I'm really looking forward to your contribution to the topic!"*

As with all moderating, you will find your own style that works for you. We do want to encourage you to act like a real person, just as you would in person. You *want* people to *want* to help you. This is one very, very big difference from a survey. If you seem remote or too formal, that approach is likely to diminish your results.

To probe or not to probe, that is the question

You can definitely probe and ask follow-up questions. The technology has made this much easier over time. Most platforms will provide some way of flagging down a participant and asking him or her to respond to a follow-up question. For example, you can send them a message with a link to the question you are following up on.

Moderators often start extended-time discussions by probing a lot, then shift their approach to less frequent probing as the participants gain experience.

Treat participant energy as a scarce resource

It's a good idea to treat follow-up questions as if you have only a very limited number you can use, and you must use them only when really important. Here's why: if participants are starting to engage with each other, they will do that less if you are constantly butting in.

Not only that, but asking people to go back to something they said before is sort of like trying to rewind a conversation by hours or days – people have moved on. Their energy is now somewhere else. So you spend a lot of participant energy asking them to go back. When people do go back, their responses are often not worth the cost in energy.

If you need to post a follow-up question, try to do it as quickly as possible after the participant's first comment on the topic. For example, the participant says something like, *"Yeah, I hate that too."* You want to say something like, *"Tara, can you say what specifically you hate? Please expand on your comment a bit more."* With any luck, Tara will see your question while she is still logged in.

By making it clear what you are looking for in the way of detail, both with direct requests and with feedback, you can avoid the need for a lot of follow-up questions.

The virtual head nod

Probing does have one clear benefit – it shows people you are listening. And listening is hugely important. Participants see what you say, and see whether you are listening and understanding them or not.

Paraphrasing or summarizing is typically discouraged as a practice in qualitative research. It can have a place as a way to show people you are listening and you get it. If you don't have a definite need to follow-up for additional detail, you could restate what you are hearing. *("I see that some people are finding the maintenance procedure really time consuming and frustrating. Others have not had as much trouble. I'm really learning a lot from what you are telling me.")* This approach generally results in feedback from the participants that they really felt "heard," which is so important. Who wants to talk to an empty room? The cautionary note is to hold off on a comment like this until most people have responded. So it is not really a follow-up, it is an acknowledgment.

The virtual head nod is even shorter – just an indicator that I'm there, reading and listening. ("Hi everyone, I don't have any follow-up questions, just want you to know I am reading and listening here . . .")

The challenge

Clients distracted by other work may log in and read something intriguing that happened earlier in the week. Then they want you to post a follow-up question.

To keep everyone happy, you may choose to bring this kind of thing back in with a fresh topic later on, rather than ask people to go back. To some extent, your own judgment about the importance of the issue to the overall project has to come into play. If the inquiry is important, you are probably better to reframe and post a new question, because you may not get much of a response to a follow-up question.

What about activity-based platforms?

Some of the newer platforms are called "activity based," and seem to require less active moderation than the basic threaded discussion approach. The platform itself provides more rewards in the form of completion tracking, and more variety in terms of the look and feel of each activity. As the platform designs get better, you may find you need to spend fewer hours in active moderation.

At the same time, as the researcher who will be conducting the analysis and writing up the report, you are well advised to keep up with everything that is happening, even if you do not need to add a lot of follow-up questions. The data can build quickly, and it helps to see it occur in real time. You will find that by gauging incoming content you will get a sense of the pace and energy around certain topics, which only helps you interpret what people are saying.

CHAPTER 11

Moderating Web Meetings

[Hosting an intimate party]

The conference call and webinar have become so popular because they solve a fundamental challenge – getting people together easily when we are not all in the same place. The traditional qualitative approaches to groups and interviews have usually involved travel, either for the moderator or the participants. Telephone interviews and telephone focus groups are one alternative. A variety of web tools will let you add a show-and-tell element, and web-video makes it a virtual face-to-face group.

The number of platform options are increasing continually, and by the time you finish reading this chapter there will likely be more. So we'll be talking about these tools fairly generically. In addition, the main mode of communication is something very familiar – the human voice. We're not going to tell you how to create a basic interview guide or group discussion guide, but instead focus on the elements that may be different from what you are used to doing.

Times and Sizes

Moderators using these methods frequently tend to prefer smaller groups.

For shared video, three to five people is very comfortable, allowing you to really see each individual's face. With six or more people, you may start to encounter slowdowns, and the individual images are smaller due to the limited real estate on a computer monitor.

One-on-one video interviews work well for 45 minutes to an hour, since every question is directed at the same individual. In comparison, a video group works best for 1.25 hours to 1.5 hours, allowing time for everyone to respond.

In our experience, longer sessions do not add value. Participants on video in a group setting are each front and center and need to listen and watch the conversation carefully, with fewer psychological breaks than in an in-person group. By keeping group sizes small, you can cover the necessary ground without going too long into over time.

Audio-only interviews and groups should run for a similar duration. Our preference is for smaller groups, but some moderators find this method effective with as many as six or eight participants. This is as much about personal comfort level in managing the group as it is about the technology. Keep in mind that focus group math applies in every situation where only one person can respond at a time.

These methods work very well for B2B participants, but consider whether there is any advantage to creating a group versus running individual interviews.

TRAVEL TIP   Doing the math

For real-time online projects, only chat is multi-synchronous. Online interviews that have participants responding via audio or video means only one person can respond at a time. This means that "the math" for figuring the duration of a group works the same as it does in a face-to-face focus group environment.

Total time – moderator talk time = time for respondents.

Time for respondents / number of topics / number of people = minutes per topic per person.

The larger the group becomes, the fewer minutes of participation from each respondent is possible.

In a 75-minute group with 5 people, if the moderator talks for just 15 minutes, you are down to just 12 minutes for each individual to speak. If you want them to respond to 6 topics, you are down to 2 minutes per topic.

One way to enhance your data collection using real real-time web-enabled methods is to leverage activities that can be done simultaneously. This can include polling questions used cleverly (e.g., finish this sentence . . .) and may include markup activities. You could do a picture sort activity asking for responses in the chat window, for example, where people type in the codes for the images they choose. You could even ask participants to complete activities before or after the group discussion.

Technology Considerations

Recruiting to a video interview is not much different than recruiting for any other qualitative project. There are just a couple of potential issues, involving the technology for your participants.

Like other interview tools, some web-meeting platforms require a download on the participant's end of things. If you are using this kind of platform, make sure your participants do the download in advance. When you send the invitation and log-in details, they can use the link early to test their system.

For participants who are working inside a major corporation, be aware that they may not be able to download anything on their workplace computer. The solution is to either use a platform that does not require a download, or ask them if they will participate from a home computer that is outside the corporation's firewall. Even if no download is required, it is a good idea to ask people to do a quick compatibility test, or to have a backup plan. Making these specifics clear at the recruiting stage is helpful.

The same factors hold true for adding video. The participants need some form of camera. This might be a webcam they plug into their desktop computer, a camera built into their laptop, or a camera built into their smartphone or other mobile device. In the past, you may have needed to send out a webcam to participants, but today you can likely screen for camera access during recruiting.

TRAVEL TIP   Do you have a camera?

While it is true that more people today have access to webcams and similar devices than in years past, be aware of whom you're excluding from your study by screening for this requirement. We suggest asking whether respondents have the right equipment, but not necessarily screening out qualified participants who don't have something suitable. Be prepared to send eligible recruits a camera to participate because eliminating them from consideration will skew your study.

Full service *versus* DIY

If you are using a full-service platform, some or all of the following activities will be done for you. The operator will get the participants on the line before the start of the session or call, and resolve any technical problems before the call starts. Some services may even be able to replace a missing participant at short notice, depending on their involvement in the recruiting. If there is a technical problem during the session, they will be on-point to deal with it, not you. Sometimes the technical problems are as simple as asking the participant to refresh their screen – but they do this all the time, so they can quickly work through the options to troubleshoot. If people lose their call connection and dial back in, the operator can deal with all of this while you carry on.

During the research event, the operator will also (depending on your preference) assist you in other aspects of the session. Here are a few things an operator may be able to do for you:

- Set up a private chat window for the observers.
- Set up a private chat window for participants to send you messages.
- Load stimuli on to the whiteboard.
- Change stimuli from one set to another mid-session.
- Load markup tools like highlighters, and even remind you how to use them.
- Load any instant polls or similar activities.
- Ensure the recording is turned on.
- Mute and unmute lines of participants and client observers.
- Change the display to focus on the face of the speaker (for video).
- Send you a link to the recordings at the end of the session.

A lot will depend on your experience, and how much tolerance there is for a bumpy ride here and there. There is a cost to having an operator assist you, but in our experience it has been well worth the price, especially if you feel you will have your hands full just managing the research interaction.

Video *versus* no video

A phone call is already an intimate form of communication, especially one-on-one. Having no need to look at the camera frees people to explore their mental world with their eyes, looking for memories or ideas.

Whether your participants are on camera or not, the client observers are seeing and hearing exactly what you are seeing and hearing, with the exception of any moderator controls. So the experience is rich for observers, either way.

Video does allow you to see the face of the participant. This often makes us feel we have some additional insight into their reactions, and gives them more avenues of expression. As the moderator, you also have more avenues of expression.

You can also ask participants on camera to show you something in their world other than their face. This might be their office, their closet, their filing cabinet, or anything else they can get into the camera screen. This is one time where mobile is a bonus, not an impediment. However, people will also pick up their laptops and move them around – it can be a bit lurchy, but informative!

Another big advantage of video is that it requires a bit more engagement, and is a bit more interactive than other online methods. There is less danger that your interviewees will get distracted by their email during your call, because you are watching them.

VOIP *versus* cellular *versus* landline

Many platforms provide Voice Over Internet Protocol (VOIP) as one of the voice communication options. While these services are steadily improving, we have learned that so far, nothing beats the reliability of a landline. However, on a long distance call, you may feel the landline option is too costly.

An advantage of VOIP is that the platform "knows" who is speaking. Newer platforms will help you easily identify the speaker by telling you which line is open. The open line is selected by the platform based on voice-activation. Or you can mute all lines except the individual you want to speak. These tools can be very helpful in managing a group situation.

Many people will just assume they can do this interview or group from their handheld, which is true. Be prepared for background noise, especially if they use their speakerphone option. Be prepared for dropped calls. If they tell you their battery is about to die, be ready to give them a different alternative. Better yet, include a reminder for participants to charge their devices in your email instructions. Trust us, all of these things have happened!

Another tip is to ask people to plan to be in a quiet place. Otherwise you may find yourself conducting an interview with someone in a coffee shop, hair salon, dentist office, or worse.

For yourself, make sure your own audio pickup will work well. This might be a microphone that is on your webcam, or it might be on your headset. But make sure you can be heard clearly on the other end. Keep in mind that several people on speakerphones at the same time often creates a lot of white noise on the call. Your platform (or your operator) will often be able to mute people who are not speaking, which can help alleviate this problem.

TRAVEL TIP   Setting up your own video camera

If you have conducted any video calls with people using a laptop, you will find that they are often zooming in and out of the picture as they move the screen to see you, then realize you can't see them, then adjust the screen again. This is okay for the interviewee, but not acceptable for the moderator.

You want people to see your face in a good light, to have relatively few distractions behind you, and to feel like your eyes are on them all the time. If you are looking at your notes (i.e. the guide) or looking at their image on screen, you will not seem to be looking at them. As one researcher put it, "There is nothing quite as distancing as a webcam moderator who is looking down all the time."

Moderators have told us about a variety of interesting set-ups to resolve the challenge of camera setup and most solutions were jerry-rigged. Your goal is to get the camera in the middle of your monitor screen if possible. Using your trusty moderator supplies (masking tape, Velcro, rulers, mini-tripods, stacks of books, etc.) you should be able to make this happen with a detachable webcam. If you are using a laptop, you want to get the camera just below eye level using a stack of books or similar.

If you can stick your guide up at eye level, that's also a good idea. You can have a copy open in a window immediately below the video display on your monitor. It might be on a second monitor, or it might be stuck up in front of you with some masking tape. This is just another place to practice those creative problem solving skills!

Be well lit, but avoid glare. Don't sit with a window behind you, and you may need to close your blinds. A desk lamp can be reorganized as a spotlight. Find an optimal distance from the camera (or adjust the camera zoom if you can) and give people a friendly face but not looming into them. Be cognizant of what is visible behind you, and whether it is distracting, or potentially even a resource to be used in quickly establishing rapport. We have also heard moderators suggest that you prepare your face as you would for a television interview – brighter makeup, ensure hair out of face, etc.

While we are at it, ensure you are not going to be distracted with other phones ringing, beeping or tweeting alerts of some kind, or even your own email. Just close it down, mute it, or move it to another room. Stick a sign on your office door to alert well-meaning visitors.

Video interviews do offer a bonus worth noting: only your top half is visible (unless you stand up, of course), so take advantage and wear something comfortable.

Sending Instructions

Whichever platform you use, you'll want to send instructions to invited participants in advance of the discussion, preferably several days before as a courtesy, so they can confirm the date and time on their calendars, reply with any questions, and test the facility link for any issues. You can ask a full-service platform provider to do this, give the information to the recruiter, or just send it out yourself. If you have the option to send out electronic meeting invitations that people can easily add to their own electronic calendar, that's a simple way to make it easy for both of you, depending on your target group, of course.

Be aware of time zones and changing time zones every spring and fall. One of the big advantages of these methods is the ability to instantly cross time zones, but it's easy to confuse people. We've found free online tools very helpful in planning.

However you send out information, it's a good idea to: a) use a single email address for all of it, and b) ask for a response so you know for sure they got the message. Coordinating all of this with your recruiter is a good idea, so that you aren't both pelting people with emails and causing confusion.

Observers

You will want to send the same type of information to your observers, telling them when and how to access the video discussion.

You may exchange a few words with the observers before the session starts if you wish, or you may prefer to stay focused. Some moderators are comfortable assuming their clients will remain silent on a call. That has always seemed a bit risky to us, but is an option. The preferred method is to mute their line once the session starts, then unmute their line after the participants have signed off.

If you are using an operator to assist you (i.e. full service platform support), this part is easy, because they manage it for you.

You can easily find yourself doing instant debriefs with your client observers after each session. If you didn't plan for this in your schedule, it can become a bit of a strain as you rush to get organized for the next call, take a bio break, and so forth. You may also be paying for operator charges that you didn't anticipate. On the other side of things, this kind of interaction is tremendously valuable to the client and to the quality of the research. You may decide on the fly to eliminate some concepts, bring back some old ideas, ask some different questions during the wrap-up, and so forth. So do consider this element in your call scheduling. You might decide to allow time between every second or third call, rather than every call. If you keep recording, you can now get this discussion transcribed, and potentially simplify your reporting process.

Disclosure

Just as you would with a recorded telephone interview, you want to quickly cover those required disclosures at the beginning of the call, as well as the presence of observers. We have had situations where people were not comfortable having the observers listen in. These were individuals who were unusually sensitive to their privacy or felt their voice alone was identifiable. If this happens, just verbally instruct the operator to close the observer lines, (i.e. take the observers off the call) and tell the observers you will be in touch after the interview.

If an interviewee has cold feet about being recorded, then you will have to make a decision on the spot as to whether or not you want to continue. Concerns about observers and recording should be avoidable by making clear disclosures at the time of recruiting. This sort of thing would not happen in a focus group facility, but the phone is their own territory, and every now and again people will surprise you. Faced with a reluctant participant, with a low incidence recruit, you may choose to carry on, and just take really great notes in the interview instead of having a recording.

Moderating

Your discussion guide will follow the same format as you would use in any one-on-one interview or small group discussion, and your timings will be similar. You are still going to set the tone and put people at ease, as well as covering some simple material at the beginning to get people relaxed. You will want to do some introductions, just as you would in face-to-face. Depending on your target, you will want to allow more or less time for this. If you sense they are still getting used to the process, just slow it down a bit.

Like any live event, do try to leave time in your guide to explore the unexpected; this is often where the rich insights lie.

Before the official video call starts, it's a good idea to show people you are "in the room." The operator can have you muted, and you can be organizing your desktop or getting your notes together. You might make a quick wave and smile, but then go back to your preparation for the call. It's another way to put people at ease. Think of it like a quick visit to the waiting room at a focus group facility – you say hello, tell people you will be starting shortly, and then go about your business setting up. Whether you are working with an operator assistant, or doing this on your own, decide on your process early in the project and use the approach that seems to be working best.

Managing the visuals

Anything you can put on the virtual whiteboard you can use as a stimulus. It is usually easy to work with a PowerPoint, but other options will be possible as well. (Refer to Chapter 8 for more on this topic.)

- Video
- Images, e.g., storyboards or advertising graphics
- Projective activities including sentence completion, picture sorts, metaphors, etc.

You can also use the platform as a virtual flipchart if you wish. This can be done in two ways. The first way is to use the whiteboard to capture text, or use markup tools (highlighters, arrows, circles, etc.) to illustrate something. The second way is to share your desktop, and capture the notes while typing into a blank document. You will want to have this set up in advance, and this is another good reason to close down other programs you will not be using during the session.

Remember to allow a few seconds to be sure that the participant's screen is actually showing the stimulus. A good practice is to just get particpants to tell you, starting early in the session, when they can see something. If you are unsure, ask "What are you seeing," not "Can you see it now?"

If you run into a situation where the visuals are simply not there for what-ever reason, then be prepared to either do a screen share, or in the worst case, email the stimuli or reschedule the call. Not every call can be easily resched-uled, however, and more than once we have emailed PDF decks of imagery to interviewees – not a great idea if these are top secret ideas, but workable for many other things. Like in-person groups, live video groups will require you to think on your feet.

Managing the audio

It is important to remember that most electronic audio will only transmit one "channel" at a time. If you've ever experienced the situation on a conference call where you are trying to speak and you can't seem to get into the call, you know how this works. As the moderator, this means you need to actually cease speaking and leave pauses for responses. The recording is not going to pick up multiple speakers.

If you are not using video, you need to pause in silence while people are thinking. They are seeing these stimuli for the first time. If the person on the other end has a preference for introversion, they are not going to be able to rapidly react. With video, you can see them thinking, but in an audio only environment, you need to manage your pacing. What may seem slow to you, especially after the first few calls, may feel like blinding speed to the interviewee or group.

Where you have a group, set the pattern early for how people will interact. You can call on them individually, changing up your order from time to time. This reduces some spontaneity, but avoids those moments where people are waiting politely for others, then try to chime in all at once.

As noted earlier, if you are using VOIP, the platform may signal who is speaking. If you don't have this and have participants on an audio-only line, you will be trying to distinguish among the voices on the call. The platform may also let you mute all or unmute specific individuals. This can help you focus on one individual for a response.

While platforms may allow individuals to "raise their hands," we haven't found this to be all that useful in interviews. Instead, consider the chat option.

Adding chat

If you have chat capabilities in the web meeting platform you are using, you can use this to help you manage the interaction. You can set up a chat window where participants can message you directly. If you let them message each other, you could wind up with side conversations, probably best avoided to keep the group focused. But if they can message only you, this window can be helpful in letting you know someone has a different idea, disagrees, or is having trouble getting into the conversation.

As with all moderated interactions, you want to show people what is expected by getting them to do it successfully as early as possible. Early in the call, have people send you a message so they know how to do it, then suggest good ways of using that capability to communicate privately with you.

Website and Software Usability

A common use of streaming video in research is to conduct website usability and software usability studies. There are now so many different approaches to this that you will want to plan your strategy according to your needs and objectives, and your view on what constitutes a good usability project.

There are an increasing number of platforms that will allow you to capture some or all of the following:

- The user's live movements on a desktop, either with the software or with the website.
- A heatmap showing user interaction with the website.
- Video and audio of the user while they are doing the assigned tasks.
- Eye tracking using a fixed or mobile device.

This is something of a specialty area, and the technology supporting this type of work is changing rapidly. Mobile devices to support eye-tracking are relatively new, while the other aspects are not.

The ability to capture interactions on a mobile device is one area that is evolving quickly, so think carefully about how you will manage the participant's interaction before submitting your research design:

- How to ensure your participant has and is using the device you want them to use, whether that is a desktop, a smartphone or a tablet.
- How to capture their actions as well as their reactions.
- What forms of data you want captured, including click-tracking or simply video of their actions.

There is no substitute to journeying with an experienced traveler, and this is an area where we encourage you to solicit the input of experienced peers before embarking on this adventure.

CHAPTER 12

Transcripts and Analysis

[We're done! Or are we?
Unpacking after the trip]

You've had an exciting tour and as you wave goodbye to the passengers, it seems like you should be able to catch a break and put your feet up with a tall, cold adult beverage. As you take the first refreshing sip, you will want to congratulate yourself for your advance planning of how you will handle all the data.

Stephen Covey's advice to "begin with the end in mind," is very relevant for online qualitative researchers. Your task of managing your data will be made much easier if you have thought about it along the way.

Fieldwork tends to gather all the glory in qualitative. It's exciting; it's a rush of new information, and it's the culmination of a lot of trip planning. But it is after the fieldwork is complete that the real value of the qualitative research consultant comes into play. Like archeologists, we sift through everything, holding bits of this or that under a magnifying glass, seeking unseen patterns and stories in the data that will address the objectives and deliver the needed insights to our clients.

Some forms of online qualitative are not very different than face-to-face in terms of data. A web-enabled discussion will give you recorded audio, and web video interviews will give you recorded video and audio. Since these events occurred primarily with voice as the means of communication, the quantity of resulting data you have will be very similar to face-to-face. You might choose to get a transcript, or might choose to simply deal with the recorded archive for analysis.

The focus of this chapter will be on the areas where there is a major difference in the type of data you receive. Online focus groups will yield a text transcript that is many times longer than the equivalent transcript for a two-hour focus face-to-face group. A discussion forum extended over even a few days will also produce a tremendous amount of text transcript. You may also have multi-media output to deal with, such as whiteboard markups, participant photos and videos, and visual projective activities you created and fielded using a whiteboard. This chapter will show you the different forms of text transcripts, and make some suggestions about multi-media output.

To give you an idea of how the volume of data differs, here are a couple of examples drawn from our own project archives. Some topics are naturally more engaging than others, and inspire people to say (write) more. The examples shown here are all for consumer projects. B2B projects can sometimes be longer, because the topics require more detail to discuss. There is no hard and fast rule. However you can expect to have anywhere from one-and-a-half to four times the data from an online approach, as compared with in-person.

Data Comparison Across Methodologies

Format	Face to face focus group	Text chat group	Discussion forum	Discussion forum	Individual diaries
Duration	Two hours per group	90 minutes	3 days	1 week	5 days
Number of participants	15 participants in 2 groups	18 participants in one group	60 participants in 5 groups	10 participants in 1 group	10 participants
Words in transcript (includes moderator questions)	11,000	18,000	88,000	33,000	15,000 Plus 79 photos and 46 videos
Transcript words per participant	733	1,000	1,466	3,300	1,500
Hours participants expected to contribute	2 hours	1.5 hours	2 hours	2 hours	2 hours

Go Get Your Data

You may choose to use some of the analysis and data manipulation tools that are available inside the platform to conduct your analysis. But you will also likely want to download and archive most of your data, in its varied forms. Make sure you obtain everything you might need before your access to the platform disappears. Some platforms offer free archiving, others offer archiving for a fee. If you don't have a lasting archive, your data will disappear after the project is over.

Here are a few of the things you will want to do with your data:

- Download the transcript in every format available.
- Download the transcript using a variety of filters to organize the data, e.g., by segment, by individual participant, by topic, by tags, etc.
- Download all multi-media files.
- Download a list of participants and any profiling information or segment assignments.

Many platforms offer transcript coding tools. If you have coded your transcripts (discussed later in this chapter), your coding should come along with the transcript when you download it. You may not need to download a list of participants and segment information, or you may find this easier than dealing with the final recruiter grid. This will be particularly true if you discover and assign segments during the project, or based on early analysis.

Platforms can vary widely in what they provide for tools and coding capabilities as well as transcripts. What follows relates to the options we have seen most often, but new tools and capabilities are constantly coming along, so be sure to ask up-front.

If there will be a lot of files, a lot of images, and so on, figuring out a simple folder and file naming convention will help you avoid a situation where you have a ton of information but aren't quite sure who it came from. If you have a lot of downloading to do, an analyst or assistant can be helpful. Some files may already have a filename (within the platform) that includes the participant name information, the group, and the specific assignment or question involved.

Text transcripts

You will usually have a few options for the transcript, including a text option and a spreadsheet format, and sometimes an HTML format.

- HTML
- Spreadsheet – Excel or CSV (Comma Separated Values)
- Text – Word or similar

The HTML format will open in a browser, and you may wonder what to do with this in order to save it and share it with clients. There are multiple ways to save a web page as a file, and you can search on these terms ("Save a web page as a file") to find out how to do it in your browser of choice, and see the various options explained. If you have PDF creation capabilities on your computer, you have another option – simply print the web page to a PDF file, which will capture all the formatting you see. You can also copy the full page and drop it into a blank Word document.

Images participants have uploaded in the transcript are usually preserved in the HTML format, except for video.

As you see what is available under the hood of your chosen platform, you will find that different formats capture images differently, and organize the text responses differently. Your platform provider will help you understand your options of course, although the geeks and perfectionists among us will likely prefer to tinker until we get what we want.

Before you release the text transcript

Be sure you have deleted any identifying information from the transcripts before you release these to clients. For example, capturing the specific geo-location of your participant is a nice feature of some discussion forums and mobile apps, but should not be available in anything that a client receives. You wouldn't give them the participants' addresses, so don't give them the neighborhood location.

This does not need to be onerous, just a quick check and some selected deletions will do the trick.

Video

If you have a lot of video, you may be able to edit and manage the video directly inside the platform, a nice bonus. If you need to deal with the video outside the platform, you will need to use some kind of video editor. Fortunately, simple video editing software is standard on both Mac and PC.

Video files will not download along with the transcript, so be sure you have all the video files you need, appropriately labeled.

There are few things as powerful as video clips to capture insights, but be forewarned that video editing is a very time consuming task. If there is a lot of video to process, and you want to create highlight clips for your client, you are well advised to have help from a videographer or video editing service. Discuss your situation with them, explain how much data you have and what you want as a finished product, and seek their advice as to the best way to approach the task within your time and budget constraints.

Keep in mind that you need to honor the anonymity commitments you made to the participants when you are sharing video. You may need to find a way to blur or pixelate the video, or remove voices, to preserve participant anonymity, depending on what you disclosed and what commitments you made to participants. Current ethical research guidelines are quite clear that you need specific disclosure if you plan to release identifiable images or video.

Once you have the video all ready to go, you need to decide how you are going to share it with your client. The files are generally too large to simply email, so you will want to consider a file-sharing service. Fortunately, there are many of these to choose from. Or, you can use your own video hosting service, which will permit you to password protect the videos and control access. If your non-geek brain is reeling, take a breath – none of this is as complicated as it might sound. These are all cloud solutions that are easy to use.

Whiteboards and mark-up tools

If you used some cool interactive tools in your project, such as whiteboards or markup tools, you will want to capture all of this information as well, in order to analyze it.

In the early days of these tools, you pretty much had to use a screen capture to get the graphics out. We can all be grateful those days are mostly gone.

To understand what we mean, consider the idea that you showed five different visual treatments for a package design. Assume you asked each participant to put down up to five markers on each stimulus. They may have chosen different colored markers to indicate positive or negative, and made brief comments on each marker they placed. The graphic below gives you an idea what one individual's responses might look like.

Package Q

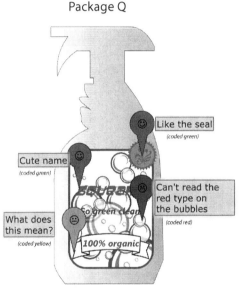

For example, some markup tools will let you look at a single individual's answers, answers for one part of the stimulus (e.g., the top right quadrant), answers for a specific segment, positives together, negatives together, and so forth. Depending on the size of your group, you might want to download all of the images, a few samples to illustrate, or perhaps none of them.

Whiteboard exercises are generally very similar. You might have created a quadrant exercise, for example, asking each participant to allocate a brand logo to each quadrant, and then comment on the rationale.

Usually, you will want to come at this data in two ways, as individual data and as aggregated data. Individual responses will let you connect what people did with the interactive graphic, e.g., how Maya sorted the brands, and what their comments say about the activity. Aggregated data will let you look for high-level patterns across all participants and across sub-groups of participants, e.g., differences with new homeowner segment.

Combining across groups

If you have been running a bigger project with multiple groups, you may encounter a different challenge – there may be no ability to analyze across groups. For example, let's look at a study where you have three segments of 15 participants for a total of 45 people. You put each segment in its own group, but the design of topics and activities is essentially the same across the three groups.

While you can find ways of merging the text commentary, just as you would with any text transcript, you may not be able to merge the analysis of interactive graphic tools.

The worst case scenario is that you have 45 individual graphics to deal with, just as you would with something like an in-person collage activity. However, in the online environment, it's easy to get carried away with these markup exercises; we are speaking from experience here, it is EASY to capture mountains of data! You might have people marking up a dozen or more individual concepts, and you have each of these across each of the three groups, leaving you with literally hundreds of individual marked-up graphics or whiteboard sorts to review and analyze.

Best case, you can use a heat-mapping analysis tool in the platform that will help you look at the aggregate data, seek patterns, and support those with individual verbatim quotes.

If you anticipate having a lot of data to analyze across different groups, some clever planning up front may save you a lot of time later on.

Sorting and ranking activities

If you used some kind of sorting or ranking activity in your project, you will need to extract this information as well. You may be able to get some basic counts and sorts from the platform, such as how many times image K was selected by the group or by a given segment.

This type of information will not likely be in the transcript, although you may be able to download a separate table or other output.

If the visual presentation of the activity is important, you may wish to capture a screen shot of the activity as the participants saw it.

Working with Transcripts

There is no magic bullet for working with qualitative data, even when it arrives already digitized. Text analyzing programs are progressing rapidly, but we have not yet seen anything that will seriously substitute for your own hard work in figuring out what you learned, organizing those learnings in a meaningful way, and making recommendations to your client.

Obviously there are lots of approaches, and any one of them may work for you. Between the two of us, we have probably tried them all. From index cards to highlighters to codes on walls and whiteboards to sticky notes to the latest 'free' text analyzer program. We all want to be efficient without reducing the added value we can provide as qual researchers.

The rest of this section will look at:

- What coding is, and how to use it.
- The tools and approaches you can use to help you through this work.
- Ways to tackle the volume of data.
- Tips and tricks.

Threaded *versus* time-coded transcripts

There is one important difference between text chat transcripts and other text transcripts from online qual studies: text chat transcripts are not threaded.

A text chat transcript can feel a bit unruly – it is conversational text among fifteen to twenty participants, with each comment being one or two sentences long.

Real-time Chat Transcript

9:15:05	**Moderator: What, if anything, would you specifically do to improve this site and why ?**
9:15:10	adam: I would expand the size of the student profile
9:15:12	barb: I agree.
9:15:15	**Moderator: Adam, why?**
9:15:17	leo: maybe use a different picture so it doesn't distract from the rest of the page
9:15:18	leslie: would move the information bar all the way to the left
9:15:20	lori: move the navigation
9:15:23	**Moderator: Barb, with whom do you agree and why?**
9:15:23	amy: oo i agree with adam
9:15:24	tara: i agree, addresses are important
9:15:30	**Moderator: Leslie, why to the left, can you elaborate?**
9:15:37	**Moderator: Lori, to where would you move the nav bar?**
9:15:40	lori: to the left hand side
9:15:45	**Moderator: Amy, can you explain more?**
9:15:48	lori: it is more intuitive
9:15:49	ted: i'd put the navigation bar to the left or at the top of the page
9:15:55	**Moderator: Tara, why are addresses important?**
9:15:55	barb: expanding the student profile: I think the most helpful information you can get when looking into schools is info from current students
9:15:56	terri: I don't like that the sections like in the news and upcoming events are where they are
9:16:05	**Moderator: Ted, why to the left or top?**
9:16:06	leslie: the address is important!
9:16:07	scott: i agree
9:16:11	**Moderator: Terri, why so?**
9:16:18	**Moderator: Scott, can you tell me more?**
9:16:20	terri: those headlines are not bolded enough...or noticeable
9:16:21	adam: I feel like the top column picture may be a little too large
9:16:30	ted: and put more info on the student/student life
9:16:31	adam: I almost thought that was the whole home page at first

In text chat, every text input is time coded and comes out in chronological order. The moderator may have asked question 3 and some participants are still answering question 2. Participants might have an additional thought that they post after the conversation has moved on. Everything, from moderator probes to private messages, will show up in the order it appeared on the screen. You will need to be cognizant of this when you are doing your analysis, and may choose to do some flagging or coding while your memory is fresh.

In a threaded discussion, the answers are always attached to the question, regardless of when the question was asked or answered. You can use the time codes, but everything posted will be linked to a question or previous comment.

Threaded Discussion: Spreadsheet Format

	A	B	C	D	E	F
1	Section Position	Section Title	Question Position	Question Title	Question Body	Message Body
539	4	Open Discuss	6	Training	What is the best way tc	I also ask friends and family on their opinions as well as reading dog magazines and asking the vet
540	4	Open Discuss	6	Training	What is the best way tc	I think the best way to train a dog is treats lol. Who doesn't like treats when you are 3 lbs? Any good behaviour and I give him treats.
541	4	Open Discuss	6	Training	What is the best way tc	When Angie taught Molly to do her tricks she used treats and positive re-enforcements. When Molly shows good behaviour i say good Molly, when she shows bad behaviour i yell {haha} and she runs! Either that or down in her kennel she goes.. Depending on what she did.
542	4	Open Discuss	6	Training	What is the best way tc	Dog magazine and asking the vet. Okay. Sounds like mostly people did not take training (i asked this same question earlier... you don't need to answer twice...[IMAGE: /images/emoticons/1.gif]}
543	4	Open Discuss	6	Training	What is the best way tc	Repetition. Rewards. Continuity. Patience. Good behavior is mainly praised and occasionally with treats. Bad behavior is scolded and sometimes 'time out'.

Online Format

Characteristics

Different dogs can have different characteristics.

Thinking about your dog, what characteristics are most important to you?
Are there any characteristics of your dog's breed that are frustrating now that you've been together a while?

> Posted by ▮▮▮▮. (Name of Dog/ Nom du(des)chien(s): ▮▮▮▮▮▮▮▮▮, Dog breed/ race ou type de chien(s): Doberman pinschers, Age of Dog/ Age de votre(vos) chien(s): 2 and 7) on 27 Nov 2013 12:22 PM
>
> I love the doberman for their sleek bodies. To me they are the jaguars of the dog world. I love their loyalty, devotion and determination. The frustration going forward with my breed is the not being able to dock and crop

> > Posted by Susan (Name of Dog/ Nom du(des)chien(s): Fuzzy, Dog breed/ race ou type de chien(s): Stuffed, Age of Dog/ Age de votre(vos) chien(s): 1) on 27 Nov 2013 6:56 PM
> >
> > Oh, is that a change to the rules?

> > > Posted by ▮▮▮▮ (Name of Dog/ Nom du(des)chien(s): ▮▮▮▮▮▮▮▮ Dog breed/ race ou type de chien(s): Doberman pinschers, Age of Dog/ Age de votre(vos) chien(s): 2 and 7) on 27 Nov 2013 8:50 PM
> > >
> > > Yes it is here in the matitimes.

> Posted by ▮▮▮▮. (Name of Dog/ Nom du(des)chien(s): ▮▮▮▮ Dog breed/ race ou type de chien(s): Hungarian viszla, Age of Dog/ Age de votre(vos) chien(s): Almost 14) on 27 Nov 2013 6:08 PM
>
> the characteristics that r important to me on a dog would be to be obedient, smart, friendly around people especially children and to watch over us

Preparing Your Transcript

If you want to use some coding, you will likely want to work with a spreadsheet such as Excel, so that you can sort and filter. A little tweaking can help a lot, but watch how much time you spend on this. And definitely work with a copy of the transcript, not the original!

Text chat transcript

For a text chat transcript, a good place to start is to add one column to the left of the transcript, and number each line sequentially. That way, no matter how many sorts you do, you can always get back to home base.

Then add some columns on the right that you will use for adding your coding information.

If you plan to merge your transcripts, you will want to add a column for Group number.

Discussion forum transcript

Extended discussions can produce a much greater volume of data and organizing it for effective analysis becomes more critical. For a discussion board, working with a copy of the original file, extract any columns that have useless information in them. All you really want is the name and the comment, grouped by question. You may also want to clean up any segmentation information that is there, ensuring you can sort and filter on this information.

If you plan to merge your transcripts, either separate them on separate spreadsheet tabs, or add a Group # column.

You can also have an analyst help you by taking the transcript and "piling up" the information in an easy to use way. You might just do this for part of the discussion, or you might do it for the whole discussion, depending on your needs. Here are two useful approaches.

Approach 1

Where you are testing multiple stimuli, put the stimuli across the top, one per column. Then put the participant IDs down the left hand column. Now you can easily see how one individual reacted to the whole set. And you can also easily see how everyone reacted to Stimulus A, B, C, etc. This can make it easier to identify patterns related to participant or segment characteristics.

	Stimulus A	Stimulus B	Stimulus C	Stimulus D
Participant 1	comment	comment	comment	comment
Participant 2	comment	comment	comment	comment
Participant 3	comment	comment	comment	comment

Approach 2

Where you are having a more wide ranging discussion about a topic, a different approach can be helpful. Let's say you are talking about usage and attitudes towards tissues in the home. You might have a couple of questions about shopping behavior, a couple of questions in which rooms in the home tissues appear, a couple of questions about package preferences by room type, and so forth.

Put one topic on a tab. Put one question per column. Put the individual participants down the side. And use one cell per comment per person. Even if Andre made four comments on a topic, some in response to other participants, they would still be aggregated beside the name.

We note here that one often does not have this kind of detail in an in-person focus group transcript, because the speaker is not necessarily identified. In online, you always know who made a comment.

Questions	Shopping	In the home	Rooms with tissue	Package
Participant 1	*First comment*	*First comment*	*First comment*	*First comment*
	Second comment		*Second comment*	*Second comment*
			Third comment	
Participant 2	*First comment*	*First comment*	*First comment*	*First comment*
	Second comment		*Second comment*	

Coding and flagging

Many platforms now give you some ability to code, flag, or highlight the transcript and individual comments before you download it. These codes and flags are then exported along with the transcript. When you look at the spreadsheet form of the transcript, you will likely see the codes – the ones you added in the platform – in a new column. This makes it relatively easy to sort or filter based on your coding.

As the moderator, you can also add your own observations to the discussion as it is evolving. For example, a participant may make a comment that suggests a possible tactical implication that you want to make in the report. You can add this thought immediately as a private moderator comment (invisible to participants) and it will show up clearly in the transcript.

If your project is relatively small, it may not be worth your time to code at all.

- Is there enough data to make it worth the time and effort?
- Do you need verbatim quotes for your report, or are you providing only top-line reporting?
- How will the report be used? Are some of the audiences for the report more interested in verbatim quotes than others?

What to code

Your project objectives should guide you in all your coding efforts. It is easy to start coding everything, and with so much data, you will be swimming in great quotes and wonderful stories.

Linking your coding plan to your objectives and expected report will help a lot. Putting "great quote" beside fifty verbatims will not save you a lot of time later. Outlining your report headings before you start structuring the data can be helpful. A major purpose of coding is to be able to support your findings with verbatim quotes. If your client does not particularly care about quotes, then you will not need to do as much, if any, coding.

- Try to refrain from coding every comment.
- You don't need to recreate another transcript – remember: quotes to support, not to report!
- Code key comments – the ones that made you go "ah, that's interesting."
- If all the comments are the same, select one that represents the lot and code it.
- If they are all different, select a sampling of the different viewpoints.
- Have a verbatim to support every major point you will make in the report.
- You are not looking for statistical significance.

How to code

If the project is small, it may be just as fast to print the transcript out and use highlighters. Or you can use the digital highlighting method, using PDF markup tools, or simple highlighting in Word. Some researchers copy their transcript into OneNote and use the tagging features there to code. Or you can code in Excel, setting up your transcript as described above.

Before you dive into creating codes:

- Read the transcript like a story, to bring it all back to mind.
- Review your objectives and what you think you want to discuss in the report.
- Use your guide as a road-map.

Your next step is to create a code list. You may have learned to do something similar for quantitative analysis, and the process is similar, although our purpose is qualitative. Take a sample of comments and create a list that captures the important themes from that sample. Then work through the rest of the transcripts. Your code list is organic and will change as you hone in and analyze more comments.

Working with Excel, you can sort using number codes, or filter using words – either will work. A list with number codes would look something like this:

Code List Example

100 Experience with Brand X

 110 Experience - Positive

 115 Experience - Neutral/None

 120 Experience - Negative

 130 Features that were a Surprise - Good

 140 Features that were a Surprise - Bad

200 Reactions to website

 210 favored design colors

 220 favored design layout

 230 favored design image

 240 related to message

 250 disliked design colors

 260 disliked design layout

 270 disliked design image

 280 didn't relate to message

Another approach to finding structure

For exploratory projects, your data may feel somewhat unstructured. For example, assume you have been interviewing employees from various areas of a large organization about their career aspirations and reasons for joining Company X versus Company Y. You did a lot of projective exercises as well as getting detailed stories. You have early career people and late career people, working in different areas of the firm, with different kinds of education. In this type of project, your fieldwork can uncover quite unexpected themes. In fact, the purpose of this type of project is to identify themes and motivations that are not well understood or may be largely unknown. The structure in a project like this emerges more from the data itself than from the objectives, even though it will answer the objectives.

Creating a big mind-map is one way to start chunking your data. Start as before, by reading portions of the transcripts like a story, just to bring it all back to mind. Then take some sticky notes and a flip-chart page and just start writing down one idea per sticky. Cluster your sticky notes into themes. This is just like a post and cluster exercise you might do with a group, but you are doing it just for yourself.

Now you can go back into your data and explore these themes, or create a set of codes for these themes. As you identify new themes, add to your code structure.

Coding software and resources

There are quite a few different software programs that support qualitative data analysis (QDA). Most have been created to support the rigorous requirements of the academic or social policy researcher, and are accordingly powerful and somewhat complex. Unfortunately for the marketing researcher, timelines that require speed may preclude this level of detailed coding. Those who have learned to use coding software find it can be very helpful, but it does tend to encourage over-coding the data, which then needs to be re-filtered and condensed.

Some of these tools are software that is installed on your own computer, while other tools are now being offered on a software-as-a-service (SAAS) basis. A few tools are available for free or on an open-source basis. A web search for "QDA software" will help you find the latest tools and reviews.

One particularly good resource is the Online QDA site (http://onlineqda. hud.ac.uk). The site covers theory and methodologies as well as approaches to analysis and coding, and has links to other resources. Although designed for the academic researcher, the site is quite approachable and well organized.

Keep in mind that the tools simply help you manage, structure, and code large amounts of data in an organized fashion; they do not actually analyze your data.

There are other tools that help to show off text data in different ways. Many word cloud tools are available online, e.g., Wordle.net. These can help you visualize words based on frequency of their occurrence. This can work well for research activities that generate lists of words, such as brand attributes. A web search on "text visualization tools" and "data visualization tools" will help you find others.

Writing the Report

The process of analyzing a qualitative research project and producing a report on the findings could form the basis of a whole book. So this section has to be considered a "drive by" on the topic. Fundamentally, a report on online qualitative studies is no different from any other type of qualitative research report, and the same structures apply.

- An executive summary should address the key purpose and findings in very brief form.
- Recommendations should provide a path forward.
- Project details will include the objectives, the methodology used, screening criteria, participant profiles, and similar contextual information.
- Key findings and Detailed findings will address all research objectives supported by verbatim quotes, usually organized according to themes.
- Appendices can contain additional graphics, transcripts, or other details that should form part of the formal records of the project.

An important challenge for the researcher today is that clients want condensed and summarized information, and they want it as quickly as possible;

these two goals can seem to be in direct opposition to each other. It is essential to understand your client's preferences for reporting as early as possible in the project to ensure your work is focused on deliverables that meet their actual needs.

Research outcomes are frequently used by individuals that were not part of the initial project team. For these folks, it makes sense to capture some visuals that give a flavor of the event, especially if the organization is relatively new to online methods. This might include screen shots of projective exercises, for example. It is also possible to set up the activities in your project so they will support a more graphical approach in the report, versus a text approach. For example, using a target diagram or quadrant diagram in a sorting activity.

A second challenge with the online project is the sheer quantity of data that can be produced, especially multi-media data. Text transcripts do not take up a lot of space, however captured video does. You may choose to provide your client with all of this material in digital form (e.g., on a USB memory stick or thumb drive) or through a secure cloud application, or on a secure part of your website. Or you may offer to store the multi-media data yourself, making it available, if needed, in the future.

CHAPTER 13

Conclusion

[What's next for the City of Insights?]

Online qualitative has had an interesting past, starting with the bulletin board systems and public chat rooms that were the first platforms used. We think the future for online qualitative is bright and the journey will continue. Forecasting the future is an activity fraught with risk, but we do see some clear trends.

Imagery

Qualitative practitioners know that the human brain often thinks in metaphor and we can use images to tap into different kinds of thinking. Current online tools have good imagery capabilities, but we see these continuing to grow and expand.

Social networks that are built around imagery have been tremendously popular, and new ones continue to pop up, e.g., Instagram, Pinterest, Vine, and SnapChat. While some brave pioneers have used platforms like Pinterest and Facebook directly for research, most researchers will want these capabilities integrated with, or recreated inside, a secure professional platform.

Hybrid Studies

The online-offline study design has been in use for a while, bringing people together online for some portions of the research, and bringing them together face-to-face for other portions. We anticipate more hybrid studies, particularly for advance preparation work, aka "homework" assignments. But we also see more potential for real-time and extended hybrids in various forms. For example, an extended community that also has live chat sessions.

As consumers continue to be more comfortable with technology of all kinds, there is less worry about confusing people with multiple response modalities. Several methods can be brought together to get the best strengths of each. For example, live chat can be used to run a brainstorming session, and then an ideation platform can be used to develop and evaluate the beginning ideas.

Another hybrid trend that hasn't waned is tackling both quantitative and qualitative objectives in a single study. Eight chat groups, each with 16 participants, will not only provide rich qualitative insights, but also could collect a sizeable amount of data among the same participants by posting the same survey on the whiteboard for each group.

New Recruiting Approaches

Recruiting is another part of the qualitative research process to become the target of innovation. Faster recruiting into studies can be readily enabled with online and mobile access methods combined with a panel database. Some of these research panels operate almost like social media, with invitations to participate pushed into an online "community" where interested individuals can respond. These environments will need to be evaluated against the same criteria used with quantitative access panels now, of course – how "fresh" is the participant pool, etc.

Extended Small Communities

The scope and scale of large communities is a barrier to using community approaches for some clients. However, a clever researcher can find ways to engage a smaller group over time. We are hearing about more extended communities being done with 25 or fewer individuals, which may not be robust enough for a global brand, but can deliver phased insights for smaller organizations using iterative innovation approaches.

More Ideation and Co-creation

In addition to the smaller extended communities, we expect to see more organizations embrace the idea of a consumer advisory board – a community of pre-screened customers that becomes involved in the creation and development of ideas in the spirit of co-creation. While large global brands have led the way in this area with popular crowdsourcing studies, we see consumers becoming more involved in extended innovation projects using online methodologies.

Crowdsourcing

Crowdsourcing has materialized in several forms and applications, and new crowdsourcing platforms are being offered as an alternative method for finding insights. The applications of crowdsourcing that seem proven in the marketplace can involve significant rewards for a significant amount of work, e.g., InnoCentive, or a share of the profits, e.g., Quirky.

Now that you have read this book, and have a method for classifying any new platform, you will see that these are extended-time methods using a variation of the community platform, and various modalities of response. Crowdsourcing as a method of qualitative insight is still finding its place in the toolkit.

Mobile

We will stop talking about mobile soon because mobile access will be so pervasive that it will be assumed as an essential access point. That may be overstating the case somewhat, because we still envision people using a wide variety of devices, including the sturdy desktop and laptop, for some time to come.

We don't really see mobile as a methodology, however; we see it as an access mode. It's just another gateway into the city of insights, incorporated into real-time or extended-time projects, using a wide variety of communication modalities.

Clients

While some clients still seem to see online methodologies as an alternative, rather than an option to be considered on every project, the future tide is rising. We know that client engagement in real-time projects is strong, yet in extended projects can be a challenge. Real-time is live and immediate, just like in-person research. Researchers are continuing to evolve ways to engage client teams effectively in extended projects. As more clients experience the depth of insights possible, we believe they will be as excited as we are about the power and flexibility of all the online qual approaches.

A Last Word

As our ways of traveling through the city of insights become ever more diverse, one thing is crystal clear from our point of view – it's not about the technology. All the tools are servants of insight, and need a thoughtful and creative research brain to operate them. It is you, the inquisitive researcher, who holds the key to running successful online qual studies – making the journey interesting, avoiding the potholes, and ensuring your client arrives safely to the destination. With this book as a guide, we encourage you to explore the city of insights, find new routes of interest, and expand your world!

Glossary of Terms

[Get your buzzwords and abbreviations
straight so you sound like a pro]

Activity

A research activity is a discrete task or exercise that is asked of participants in a research study. Activity-based platforms present participants with a selection of activities that the participant navigates. Activities could include anything from a group discussion, to an individual text response, a photo sort, or anything else. Discussion forums also use activities, but the structure looks and feels a little different, because the sequencing of tasks usually appears more as a sequence of topics within a threaded discussion.

Asynchronous

Research events where the participants do not need to be present at the same time are called asynchronous. In this book, extended is the same thing as asynchronous.

Avatar

An avatar is a small graphic icon that identifies the posts of an individual participant. Avatars are used in some platforms to make the environment more easily scannable and more engaging. Some platforms will allow participants to choose their own avatar from a set of avatars. Generally, a platform will use either an avatar or a photo provided by the participant, but not both.

Blinded

A blinded question is one where the participant cannot see anyone else's response until they respond. Online tools often offer this as an option when posing a question or discussion topic. The purpose of blinding a question is to get initial responses from participants that are unbiased by what others say. After posting their own response to the question, participants are then able to see what others have said, and react to those other comments. A question that never permits viewing the other responses is usually called a one-on-one question.

Some platforms use different language, such as "restricted" to refer to a blinded question.

You may also see the term "blind" used in connection with a whole project. A blinded study is a study where the sponsor is not revealed to those participating in the research.

Blogging

Blogging generally refers to a written diary tool where the participants can post at will on whatever topic is relevant. In this sense, an individual participant blog is somewhat unstructured, compared to a journal or diary. Depending on the platform and tool, the blogging tool may permit others in the study (the whole group or a specific segment) to view and comment on other participants' blog entries.

Bulletin board

Bulletin boards are also called discussion boards and discussion forums. There are many features and tools, but the basic backbone of a bulletin board or a discussion forum is a threaded discussion where the moderator poses a question and the participants type in a response. The moderator may ask follow-up questions. Participants are generally able to respond to a question more than once, and are generally also able to respond to posts that other participants have made.

This is an asynchronous or extended methodology.

City of Insights

City of Insights is an extended metaphor used throughout this book. The city is the destination: insight. There are many modes of transportation that can be used to journey to insights, which equate to the many and growing number of methodologies for conducting online qualitative research.

Community

See Insight Community

Diaries

Diaries are a written log kept by a participant. They may also be a photo or video diary, or a combination of all of these. A diary is generally private between the moderator and a single participant, even if there are others present in the study. Diaries can sometimes be set up to pose the same set of questions each day, (or each time the participant logs in) and remind the participant to answer. A bulletin board can be used as a diary by setting the question types to one-on-one mode.

Discussion forum

A friendlier and more evocative name for the technology that started life as "Bulletin Board." There are many features and tools, but the basic backbone of a discussion forum is a threaded discussion where the moderator poses a question and the participants type in a response. The moderator may ask follow-up questions. Participants are generally able to respond to a question more than once, and are generally also able to respond to posts that other participants have made.

This is an asynchronous or extended method.

ESOMAR

ESOMAR is a global society for marketing research. ESOMAR publishes the most comprehensive set of ethical guidelines related to qualitative research in all forms. www.esomar.org

Extended time

Extended time is a more user-friendly way of saying asynchronous. Extended time happens over an extended period, versus real time, where everyone is participating simultaneously in the research event.

Group effects

Group effects refers to the impact of hearing, reading, or seeing the responses of others on one's own opinion. Most online methods provide for exceptionally good control over group effects. The moderator can generally blind a question, even when the question is a reaction to a visual stimulus such as a video. This forces the individual participants to respond with their own thoughts first, before seeing or hearing what others say. It is also easy for the moderator to see in the transcript the change in comments that is created by seeing what others have said, so it is really the best of both worlds.

In text chat, responses go by so quickly that group effects are minimized. It is possible to blind a question, but generally unnecessary.

Real-time web meetings have to be managed for group influence in the same way as in-person focus groups.

Heat map

A heat map is a type of analysis tool that is used after data is gathered, typically with a markup exercise. A visual stimulus like an image is presented, and the participants put markers directly on it, showing parts they like or dislike, or where they have questions or confusion. A heat map will give the moderator a visual snapshot of the total marks and comments made. It's like looking at all of the responses at the same time. Heat map tools also generally allow for some filtering, such as looking only at positive or negative marks, or only at a specific segment of responses.

Immersive

Immersive research refers to research approaches that take the research team into the lives and context of participants so that as observers you become immersed in their world. Traditional methods of doing this include ethnography and observational research, and the online version of observational research is sometimes called netnography. In online qualitative, some of the tools that can be used to create immersive research are: diaries, journals and blogs; participant video and photo captures; extended duration research to capture more events and activities over time. While you may see the word immersive used to describe a platform, in reality, it is possible to design immersive research using many different approaches. The key distinction of immersive research is that it strives to take a holistic approach to the topic.

Insight community

Insight communities are also referred to as Marketing Research Online Communities, or MROC for short.

The term insight community can be confusing, because it has been applied to many different approaches. In general, it refers to a project that is extended over a period of time from weeks to months or even years. From our perspective, there needs to be a significant amount of uncontrolled interaction among the participants to genuinely earn the moniker "community," such as participants initiating their own discussions. This is not typical of most online qualitative projects, where the interaction is carefully designed by, and largely controlled by, the researcher. Not all platforms support participants generating their own topics of discussion.

You will see in this book that we are using the label "online community" to refer even to shorter ad hoc projects that occur on an extended discussion forum or purpose-built community platform simply for the sake of simplicity. The distinctions in the technology are rapidly diminishing, and it is just simpler to refer to these platforms as "online community platforms."

Community size can vary widely, from a few dozen individuals to thousands. As well, the expected time commitment from participants can vary widely, from participation in occasional exercises taking a few minutes, to a commitment of as much as an hour a week over an extended period.

You will also see large respondent panels referred to as communities, even when most of the research activities are quantitative in nature.

Journal

A journal is an online diary that a participant is asked to post to multiple times, typically over a period of days or weeks. A journal is usually visible only to the researcher and the individual participant, even if there are multiple participants in the study. A journal may be one activity in a larger study that also involves interactive activities.

Longitudinal

Longitudinal research occurs over a longer period of time, looking at the way an issue, topic, or usage changes over time. While longitudinal studies are most often thought of in the academic sense, online research permits longitudinal study of many topics of interest to marketers.

Marketplace community

A marketplace community is created primarily to build loyalty with consumers, and give them a place to express their interests and enthusiasms for brands. This type of community may have insight gathering as a secondary purpose. Participation is generally wide open, with no formal recruiting or screening process in place and no validation of identity. There is no incentive or expectation of active participation, and there is no active moderation.

Markup tool

A markup tool lets participants place visual markers or text on stimuli that are converted to image formats. The actual stimuli can be an image, such as a print advertisement, but can also be words shown in image form, such as a concept.

Mobile device

This could be a cell phone, but does not have to be a phone. Tablets and iPods, for example, may be able to capture images, video, or text responses for immediate (or later) upload. Platforms vary greatly in how they approach mobile data collection; however this area is improving rapidly. A key difference among platforms and apps is whether or not the app will work in the absence of an internet connection. In this book, reference to a mobile device is intended to include the broadest possible range of internet-enabled devices.

Mobile tools

A growing number of online qualitative platforms allow at least some access through a mobile device. This could be simply through a browser, if the site is designed to be responsive to the small screen environment. Or there may be an actual app that is downloaded that provides access to some tools through the mobile device.

Moderator tools

Moderator tools are capabilities provided in the platform that make the moderator's job easier. These can be tools that assist in creating the online discussion guide, helping during actual moderation, or supporting analysis. For example, the moderator will want to know which participants have responded to a given question, whether in real-time or extended-time studies. Most platforms provide tools that are only available to the moderator to assist in managing the project.

MROC

Short for Marketing Research Online Community. See Insight Community.

Multi-media

Platforms vary in their ability to work with different forms of media, including digital images, digital video, and digital audio.

Multi-synchronous

Text chat is an online methodology that is not just synchronous (real time), it is multi-synchronous. All participants can interact at the same time, in real time. This characteristic enables text chat groups to produce significantly more data than an equivalent time commitment to other real-time methods, such as face-to-face focus groups or webcam groups.

Observer

An observer in an online study is able to see, but not participate in, the research activity. Depending on the platform, they may be able to post observations or questions that are visible to other observers and the moderator, but not visible to the participants. The moderator generally has full control over observer interaction.

Offline access

Some mobile qualitative tools require an active internet connection to work (either through Wi-Fi or a cellular connection). Others provide for offline access, meaning that responses can be gathered from participants for later upload.

One-on-one

A one-on-one question is set up so that the participant cannot see other replies to the topic or question. The moderator may be looking at multiple replies for multiple respondents, none of whom can see what others have posted. This is a common option available for question types. Some platforms called this form of question "closed." See also Blind.

Online focus group

An online focus group is a real-time text chat discussion. It is often abbreviated as OLFG.

Online meeting

An online meeting is a voice and visual event that takes place using a platform designed to facilitate meetings. These platforms are generally not research specific, but can be used for research purposes. The voice connection can be via the internet or via a conference calling service (or even both at the same time). The visual portion can be a display of stimuli (e.g., image, projective exercise), but also could include screen sharing, live exploration of a website, and markup tools for participants. Some meeting platforms have limited text chat capabilities as well.

Panel

A panel in the marketing research context usually refers to a large list of potential participants that have already been initially recruited and screened, and have expressed an interest in being contacted for marketing research studies. The majority of the studies that are conducted with panels are surveys of some form; however panels can also be used to recruit participants in qualitative projects.

Panels can be of the open-access type, where any researcher may gain access to panel participants for a fee. Private panels are also maintained by some organizations that are only available for their own use. What can be confusing is when you see the word "community" used to refer to an access panel that contains many thousands of individuals, even as many as 100,000, where the primary activity of participants is responding to surveys.

Participant

It is common in the marketing research industry to refer to the users, consumers, and customers in our studies as respondents. As qualitative practitioners, we prefer the term participant as a more respectful acknowledgment of the enormous contribution participants bring to our work. They share private and personal experiences, often in the presence of strangers, and frequently provide the raw material for ground-breaking product, distribution, and marketing innovations.

Participant initiated

A participant initiated activity is something a participant can start without being asked a question by a moderator. Participant initiated activities, such as discussion topics or mini-polls or similar activities, are more commonly allowed in platforms designed for extended communities rather than one-off or ad hoc projects.

Participant profile

A participant profile provides some basic information about the individuals participating in the study. This might be simple demographic data such as age, gender, and location. Or it might be information that defines a segment, such as product usage or attitudes. A photo or avatar is sometimes attached to the profile.

Platform

A platform is a collection of tools and technologies that provide a virtual place to conduct online research in various forms and modalities.

Polling

Various platforms have polling capabilities that permit asking simple survey-like questions to the participants. Polling is available in real-time and extended-time platforms. Polling can be used to gauge overall reactions to a stimulus, but can also be used as a way to engage participants, particularly if they are permitted to see the poll results. Creative use of polling capabilities can also be used to manage group effects and support projective activities. Polling capabilities are not a substitute for an actual survey involving several questions.

Projective exercise

A projective exercise is a research activity that allows participants to "project" their attitudes, thoughts, and beliefs into a scenario indirectly, making it easier for participants to express different kinds of ideas, including negative, creative, and non-rational ideas. The concept originated with clinical psychology.

Quali-quant

Quali-quant refers to hybrid approaches of research that rely on both structured (e.g., survey) and unstructured data (e.g., free-ranging discussions). With the advent of social media listening research methods, the argument can be made that it is not the data that is either inherently qualitative or quantitative, but the analytical approach to the data.

QRC

A QRC is a qualitative research consultant, a research professional who helps clients solve business problems using qualitative research methods.

QRCA

The Qualitative Research Consultants Association, one of the professional homes of QRCs worldwide. www.qrca.org

Ratings

Some online platforms allow posts to be ranked and rated. This type of tool is used where ideation is the goal, and lets others in the study or the community vote up or vote down various ideas. Ratings can usually be turned on or off, to allow for a period of creating ideas followed by a period of ranking them.

Real time

Real time, or synchronous, refers to research events that are scheduled for simultaneous involvement by participants. The plan is for everyone to be there at the same time, whether by voice or text.

Respondent

The people who participate in surveys and qualitative research are often called respondents. Our view is that participant is a preferable term for qualitative work, because we rely on a willingness to disclose personal information, we are seeking more than simple responses, and the research is much more of an interaction than a call and response situation.

Segmenting

In the context of online qualitative, segmenting tools permit the researcher to identify sub-groups based on specific characteristics, such as demographics, product usage, or attitudes determined from a screener. Platform capabilities vary, but generally include some ability to direct segments to specific questions, and to filter responses by segment.

SMS messaging

SMS or Short Message Service is the formal name for short text messages. SMS messaging is not dependent on the internet, and is most commonly used in mobile telecommunications. SMS is often an adjunct communication for online qualitative, used for sending reminders and information to participants, as an alternative to email. Some online platforms will accept SMS messages as well, and direct the messages into a threaded discussion, blog, or journal entry.

Synchronous

Synchronous research happens in real time. All face-to-face methods are synchronous. Online focus groups (text chat), web-cam groups, and web meetings are also synchronous.

Tagging

Online research platforms often permit the researcher to mark specific participant input with tags as part of the analysis process. Tags can then facilitate finding similar content across a transcript or even multiple transcripts, depending on the platform. At the time of writing, tagging is a manual operation.

Telephone

The phone has come a long way from its early days, and could be a landline, a cellular phone, or an internet voice connection. Most of the references in this book to phone simply refer to a voice connection, through any one of these pipelines.

Text chat

A text chat is a real-time (synchronous) communication using typed text, and forms the backbone of online focus group platforms.

Text messaging

See SMS messaging.

Transcript

In online research, a transcript is generally downloadable during (extended-time) or at the end of (real-time) text chat groups. Transcripts can often be downloaded in multiple formats, including spreadsheet formats and text formats. Web-enabled meetings and web-cam groups can be recorded, but do not generally come with a transcript.

Video

Video can take many forms in online qualitative. It can be recorded on a camera and then uploaded into the platform; it can be recorded from a web-camera attached to a laptop or desktop computer directly into a platform; it can be captured using a mobile application on a handheld device or tablet. Platforms vary in their video response capabilities. Video can be used as a way to communicate with participants, as a stimulus to respond to, or as a form of participant response. With webcam groups and interviews, recorded video forms a record of the real-time event.

VOIP

VOIP stands for Voice Over Internet Protocol, and is an internet-enabled voice communication. Online meeting platforms often have VOIP capabilities.

Webcam

A webcam is a general term referring to a small camera used as a peripheral device on a computer, or built in to most laptops. However, a live video connection can also be obtained through the use of video capabilities on handheld devices and tablets.

Whiteboard

A whiteboard is a virtual version of the physical whiteboard. It is a blank screen that can be used to display images that can be moved around and sorted. It can display a still image that can be marked up with text, arrows, highlighters, and similar marks by participants. You can also use whiteboards to show video and live websites. Whiteboards can be used in real-time and in extended-time projects, either by individual participants, or by a group interacting together. Whiteboard technologies and capabilities vary.

Acknowledgments

[We're all in this together]

There are many people who bolstered our understanding and creative thinking about online qualitative research. We are sincerely grateful for the support, consideration, and teaching from our fellow members of the Qualitative Research Consultant's Association (QRCA). Overflowing with creative energy and natural curiosity, these thoughtful quallies have generously shared their experiences over the years, which further stoked our excitement of the topic.

We'd like to thank the people who were interviewed or contributed directly to this book: David Bradford, Corette Haf, Ilka Kuhagen, Betsy Leichliter, Ricardo Lopez, Pia Mollback-Verbic, Piyul Mukherjee, Susan Roth, Marian Salzman, Mary Beth Solomon, Liz Van Patten, and Amy Yoffie.

Thanks to all our vendor partners for encouraging us to think differently and designing systems to meet the unique needs of the qualitative researcher. Whether it's making that special custom adjustment to your program, or taking our frantic calls at all hours of the day or night, THANK YOU.

Our heartfelt appreciation to all the research participants, without whom we would have nothing to say. We thank you for sharing your private thoughts, honest opinions, and candid concerns about whatever we need to know.

To our publishing team, Doris and Jim, for their warm approach and continued support of not only us, but our entire industry.

To our friends and family who buoyed our spirits and kept our lives humming while we were head down in the development of this book.

And a high five to each other, for a virtual collaboration that was challenging, stimulating, and most of all, fun.

We look forward to seeing you in the city of insights!

A Roadmap

GPS works well, but sometimes you need an old fashioned roadmap. If you are new to moderating online, you will probably find useful information on every page. But once you have the big picture and need to go back into the details, here's some help to find the location you are looking for.

If you want to	See these pages
Get a quick overview of the **different kinds** of interviews and focus groups you can do online	20
See a **timeline** for a typical study launch	130–131, 132, 140, 150–153
See the definition of a **term**	191–202
Moderate a **web meeting**	158–169
Moderate in **extended time**	33, 41, 49–50, 56–57, 95–96, 132–157
Figure out how to **price** your work	73–82
Avoid the **ethical pitfalls** of online moderating	65–72, 137
Use **video** or webcams in your online moderating	18–19, 33–34, 96–106, 158, 161–164, 174
Show a concept for your participants to **markup**	22, 57, 97–98, 121, 158, 161, 169, 171, 174–176
Recruit participants	77–79, 85–86, 113–114

If you want to	See these pages
Plan **incentives**	75–77, 108–110
Moderate in **real time**	95–96, 111–133
Review the platforms and **tools** that are available to help with online moderating	14–18, 43–64, 68, 81–88, 158–159, 97–99, 102–107, 121, 158–159
Get information on **managing transcripts** after the session ends	50, 84, 170–186
See **case studies**	19, 24–26, 28–29, 30–31, 35, 37–38, 41–42, 63–64, 71–72, 83, 92–93
Learn about **mobile platforms**	35–38
Plan your **study objectives**	44–45
Know **what to ask platform providers**	51–60
View statistics on global **internet use**	86
Plan your **project**	95–96, 104–107
Organize and use **stimuli**	23, 27, 96–106, 121–122, 136, 169–170
Deal with **observers**	15, 17, 21, 49, 56, 58, 62, 83, 102, 107–113, 165–166
Consider **approaches** to **questioning**	146–149
Learn more about the **technology**	36–37, 50–60, 160–164, 169–170
Take **global studies** into consideration	15, 25, 58, 27, 83–84
See **examples** of **sessions** and **transcripts**	84, 117, 171, 178, 179, 183

About the Authors

Jennifer Dale and Susan Abbott met at a qualitative research conference. Both are active members of the Qualitative Research Consultants Association (QRCA), where each has served in a variety of leadership capacities. They share a passion for excellence and are enthusiastic practitioners of qualitative research in all its many forms. Collaborating on this book was a joyful experience, completed start to finish on a virtual basis.

Jennifer is President and CEO of InsideHeads, LLC, a full-service marketing research company conducting both quantitative and qualitative research via the web to clients across the globe. Jennifer has been at the forefront of online qualitative since 1997, when she was employed as a bright young researcher at Research Connections, Inc. She obtained her MBA in 1995 while working full-time as the Director of Marketing for Philips-Van Heusen, maker of such iconic brands as Izod and Geoffrey Beene. When not working, you'll find her hiking, kayaking, and playing with her adopted shelter pets at home in the U.S. Virgin Islands.

Susan is President of Abbott Research + Consulting, and co-founder of Think Global Qualitative, a global alliance of master qualitative researchers. Her professional focus is bringing customer insight, creative thinking and focused innovation to business challenges. She has a particular passion for customer experience design. Before launching her business in 2001, she was a vice-president of TD Bank Group, where she held diverse general management positions. When not working, she likes to paint outdoors, ride a Vespa, and pick up sparkly ideas at conferences. A previous book, *The Innovative Organization*, was published in 2006. She is based in Toronto, Canada.